Latin
FOR COMMON ENTRANCE

13+
LEVEL 3

Exam Practice Questions

Latin
FOR COMMON ENTRANCE

**13+
LEVEL 3**

Exam Practice Questions

R.C. Bass

GALORE PARK

AN HACHETTE UK COMPANY

About the author

Bob Bass taught at prep schools in Somerset, Kenya and Sussex before moving in 1987 to Orwell Park, Ipswich, where he is Head of Classics and Senior Master. He has served on the editorial board of the *Journal of Classics Teaching* and on the Council of the Joint Association of Classical Teachers. For 12 years he edited the SATIPS Classics Broadsheet, and has been IAPS' Subject Leader and then Subject Adviser in Classics. He is the Chief Setter of ISEB's Common Entrance and Common Academic Scholarship Latin papers, proof-reader for their Greek papers, and an IGCSE examiner. He is the author of various Latin and Greek resources targeted at young learners.

Every effort has been made to trace all copyright holders, but if any have been inadvertently overlooked, the Publishers will be pleased to make the necessary arrangements at the first opportunity.

Although every effort has been made to ensure that website addresses are correct at time of going to press, Galore Park cannot be held responsible for the content of any website mentioned in this book. It is sometimes possible to find a relocated web page by typing in the address of the home page for a website in the URL window of your browser.

Hachette UK's policy is to use papers that are natural, renewable and recyclable products and made from wood grown in sustainable forests. The logging and manufacturing processes are expected to conform to the environmental regulations of the country of origin.

Orders: Teachers please contact Bookpoint Ltd, 130 Park Drive, Milton Park, Abingdon, Oxon OX14 4SE. Telephone: (44) 01235 400555. Email primary@bookpoint.co.uk. Lines are open from 9 a.m. to 5 p.m., Monday to Saturday, with a 24-hour message answering service

Parents, Tutors please call: 020 3122 6405 (Monday to Friday, 9:30 a.m. to 4.30 p.m.). Email: parentenquiries@galorepark.co.uk

Visit our website at www.galorepark.co.uk for details of other revision guides for Common Entrance, examination papers and Galore Park publications.

ISBN: 978 1 471853 49 4

© Robert C. Bass 2015

First published in 2015 by
Galore Park Publishing Ltd,
An Hachette UK Company
Carmelite House
50 Victoria Embankment
London EC4Y 0DZ
www.galorepark.co.uk

Impression number   10 9 8 7 6 5 4 3

Year   2019

Typeset in India

Printed in the United Kingdom

A catalogue record for this title is available from the British Library.

Contents

Introduction

This collection of practice exercises, previously published as *Latin Practice Exercises Level 3*, is designed to provide material for pupils who have been studying Latin for at least two years, particularly those preparing for the ISEB Common Entrance examination at Level 3 and Scholarship level.

It provides extensive material for translation, both into and out of Latin, giving pupils the opportunity to revise or consolidate skills they have learnt in those courses.

The vocabulary, grammar and syntax are deliberately geared to the Level 3 syllabus for Common Entrance and also cover the Common Academic Scholarship requirements. Only two words are included which are not required for either one: **scio** and **nescio**.

The answers (ISBN: 9781510462120), including mark schemes for the exercises, are available separately. For a full list of resources available visit www.galorepark.co.uk

Nicholas Oulton
Series Editor

→ The syllabus and your exams

For Common Entrance Latin, you will sit an exam lasting one hour. You will choose one of the three levels, Level 1, Level 2 or Level 3, as agreed with your teacher.

The format of each level is the same, but the material gets harder. In each level, there are four questions worth a total of 75 marks, as follows:

Question 1 (15 marks)

A short passage of Latin will be set, on which you will be asked to answer eight to ten questions, testing your understanding of the passage. You will not be expected to write a translation of the passage, but clearly you need to have translated it in your head, in order to answer the questions.

Question 2 (30 marks)

Another, slightly longer passage will be set, continuing the story from the passage in Question 1. You will be asked to translate this passage, writing your translation on alternate lines.

Question 3 (20 marks)

Another short passage of Latin will be set, continuing the story from the earlier two passages. Questions will be set, testing your knowledge of Latin grammar and how the language works. You will not be asked to translate this passage, but again you will find it difficult to answer the questions unless you have translated it for yourself.

The questions will fall into the following types:

- From the passage give, in Latin, one example of: (an adjective, a preposition followed by the accusative, a noun in the genitive, a verb in the imperfect tense, etc.)
- **erat** (line 2). In which tense is this verb? What is the 1st person singular of the present tense of this verb?
- **pueros** (line 4). In which case is this noun? Why is this case used?
- **vocaverunt** (line 5). What does this word mean? What is the connection between **vocaverunt** and the English word *vocation*?

- **necat** (line 5) means *he kills*. How would you say in Latin *he was killing* (imperfect tense)?
  And last but not least:
- Using the vocabulary given, translate the following two short sentences into Latin.

Most candidates lose the majority of their marks on Question 3 by falling into the trap of thinking they do not need to translate the passage. They simply guess the answers. To answer a question such as 'in which case is the word **templum** in line 3?', you have to have translated the sentence in which the word **templum** is. Otherwise you will simply be guessing, particularly with a word such as **templum**, which could be any of nominative, vocative or accusative singular.

Question 4 (10 marks)

You will be set eight questions on four areas: Roman domestic life; the city of Rome; the army and Roman Britain; and Greek mythology. Each question will have two parts, part (i) and part (ii). You select **one** question, and answer both parts of it. Examples are given below:

The city of Rome

(c) (i) Tell the story of Cloelia.

(ii) Which elements of this story would the Romans have found particularly admirable? Explain your answer.

Greek mythology

(h) (i) Tell the story of Odysseus' encounter with the Cyclops.

(ii) Describe two qualities which Odysseus displayed in this encounter.

These are two of the eight questions that might have been set, labelled (a) to (h). If you had chosen to do the one labelled (c) above, you would have done both part (i) and part (ii) of that question.

→ Tips on revising

Get the best out of your brain

- Give your brain plenty of oxygen by exercising. You can only revise effectively if you feel fit and well.
- Eat healthy food while you are revising. Your brain works better when you give it good fuel.
- Think positively. Give your brain positive messages so that it will want to study.
- Keep calm. If your brain is stressed, it will not operate effectively.
- Take regular breaks during your study time.
- Get enough sleep. Your brain will carry on sorting out what you have revised while you sleep.

Get the most from your revision

- Don't work for hours without a break. Revise for 20–30 minutes, then take a five-minute break.
- Do good things in your breaks: listen to your favourite music, eat healthy food, drink some water, do some exercise or juggle. Don't read a book, watch TV or play on the computer; it will conflict with what your brain is trying to learn.
- When you go back to your revision, review what you have just learnt.
- Regularly review the material you have learnt.

Get motivated

- Set yourself some goals and promise yourself a treat when the exams are over.
- Make the most of all the expertise and talent available to you at school and at home. If you don't understand something, ask your teacher to explain.
- Get organised. Find a quiet place to revise and make sure you have all the equipment you need.
- Use year and weekly planners to help you organise your time so that you revise all subjects equally. (Available for download from www.galorepark.co.uk)
- Use topic and subject checklists to help you keep on top of what you are revising. (Available for download from www.galorepark.co.uk)

Know what to expect in the exam

- Use past papers to familiarise yourself with the format of the exam.
- Make sure you understand the language examiners use.

Before the exam

- Have all your equipment and pens ready the night before.
- Make sure you are at your best by getting a good night's sleep before the exam.
- Have a good breakfast in the morning.
- Take some water into the exam if you are allowed.
- Think positively and keep calm.

During the exam

- Have a watch on your desk. Work out how much time you need to allocate to each question and try to stick to it.
- Make sure you read and understand the instructions on the front of the exam paper.
- Allow some time at the start to read and consider the questions carefully before writing anything.
- Read every question at least twice. Don't rush into answering before you have a chance to think about it.

Exercise 1.1

Translate the following passage. Line numbers are given on the left. New words are underlined in the text and their meanings given in the margin.

The Trojan Aeneas urges his friends to abandon Troy

1 Graeci urbem Troiam delebant. multos milites
  Troianos necabant. multa templa incendebant.
  multos cives capiebant. Aeneas princeps
  Troianus erat. ubi milites Graecos in media urbe
5 stantes vidit, amicos convocavit et haec verba
  eis dixit:

  'amici, urbs nostra a Graecis capitur. in maximo
  periculo sumus. milites nostri necantur. templa
  nostra incenduntur. cives nostri capiuntur.
10 effugere debemus. arma capite! domos
  relinquite! naves parate! statim discedamus!'

  arma igitur a Troianis capiuntur. domus
  relinquuntur. naves parantur. Aeneas et amici
  prope naves conveniunt et ex urbe Troia
15 celeriter discedunt.

incendo, -ere, incendi (3) = I set on fire, I burn
princeps, principis, m. = chieftain
stantes = standing
convoco, -are, -avi (1) = I call together
a/ab + ablative = by
capitur = is being captured
necantur = are being killed
incenduntur = are being burned
capiuntur = are being captured
debemus = we ought, we must
domos = homes
discedamus! = let's leave!
capiuntur = are taken
domus = homes
relinquuntur = are abandoned
parantur = are prepared
convenio, -ire, -veni (4) = I meet

Total: 75

Exercise 1.2

1 From the passage give an example of:

  (a) a verb in the imperfect tense. (1)

  (b) a verb in the perfect tense. (1)

  (c) a superlative adjective. (1)

2 dixit (line 6). Give the person and number of this verb. Give the
  1st person singular of the present tense of this verb. (3)

3 amici (line 7). In which case is this noun? (1)

4 naves (line 11). In which case is this noun? Why is this case used? (2)

5 celeriter (line 15). Explain the connection between this word and
  the English word *accelerate*. (1)

Total: 10

In this chapter you meet verbs in what is called the **passive voice**: the subject is being acted upon.

> **Example**
> The boy is being watched.

1st conjugation

Exercise 1.3

Translate the following into English:

1 amamur.

2 laudatur.

3 vulnerantur.

4 vocaris.

5 portor.

6 liberamur.

7 nuntiatur.

8 laudamini.

9 necantur.

10 spectamini.

1 mark for each question. Total: 10

2nd conjugation

Exercise 1.4

Translate the following into English:

1 monetur.

2 videmini.

3 moveris.

4 tenetur.

5 terreris.

6 delentur.

7 videntur.

8 movemur.

9 monemini.

10 iubemur.

1 mark for each question. Total: 10

3rd and mixed conjugation

Exercise 1.5

Translate the following into English:

1 regimur.

2 ponitur.

3 capimini.

4 defenditur.

5 faciuntur.

6 mitteris.

7 traduntur.

8 occidimini.

9 vincuntur.

10 iacitur.

1 mark for each question. Total: 10

4th conjugation

Exercise 1.6

Translate the following into English:

1 auditur.

2 inveniuntur.

3 punior.

4 audimini.

5 puniris.

6 invenitur.

7 punimur.

8 audiris.

9 audiuntur.

10 punitur.

1 mark for each question. Total: 10

Exercise 1.7

Translate the following into English:

1 defendimur.

2 ducuntur.

3 deletur.

4 spectamur.

5 legitur.

6 mittimur.

7 interficitur.

8 ponimini.

9 oppugnantur.

10 puniuntur.

1 mark for each question. Total: 10

→ Translating 'by' into Latin

1 **by** + a person = a/ab + ablative

Example
The town is being attacked by the enemy.
oppidum **ab hostibus** oppugnatur.

2 **by** + a thing = ablative **only**

Example
The town is being attacked by arrows.
oppidum **sagittis** oppugnatur.

Exercise 1.8

Translate the following into English:

1 hostis militem vulnerat.

2 miles ab hoste vulneratur.

3 iuvenis librum legit.

4 liber a iuvene legitur.

5 servi cibum parant.

6 cibus a servis paratur.

7 magister pueros laudat.

8 pueri a magistro laudantur.

9 hostes urbem oppugnant.

10 urbs ab hostibus oppugnatur.

3 marks for each question. Total: 30

Exercise 1.9

Translate the following into English:

1 ego puellam amo.

2 puella a me amatur.

3 servi vinum bibunt.

4 vinum a servis bibitur.

5 Romani oppidum capiunt.

6 oppidum a Romanis capitur.

7 rex terram regit.

8 terra a rege regitur.

9 Graeci Romanos vincunt.

10 Romani a Graecis vincuntur.

3 marks for each question. Total: 30

Exercise 1.10

Translate the following into English:

1 Romani Graecos semper vincunt. (4)

2 Graeci a Romanis semper vincuntur. (5)

3 dominus servos saepe punit. (4)

4 servi a domino saepe puniuntur. (5)

5 poeta libros semper legit. (4)

6 libri a poeta semper leguntur. (5)

7 patrem amas. (2)

8 pater a te amatur. (4)

9 milites urbem defendunt. (3)

10 urbs a militibus defenditur. (4)

Total: 40

Exercise 1.11

Translate the following into English:

1 tempestas naves delet. (3)

2 naves tempestate delentur. (3)

3 hostes nos non amant. (4)

4 ab hostibus non amamur. (4)

5 discipuli magistrum amant. (3)

6 magister a discipulis amatur. (4)

7 cives regem vulnerant. (3)

8 rex a civibus vulneratur. (4)

9 puer urbem videt. (3)

10 urbs a puero videtur. (4)

Total: 35

Exercise 1.12

Translate the following into English:

1 ab hostibus spectamur.

2 hostes gladiis occiduntur.

3 a domino mittor.

4 a patre amor.

5 a magistro laudaris.

6 milites sagittis vulnerantur.

7 a servo portatur.

8 a domino liberantur.

9 a militibus capimini.

10 a rege defendimur.

3 marks for each question. Total: 30

Exercise 1.13

Translate the following into English:

1 a Romanis vincimur.

2 hastis, Marce, vulneror.

3 a puero spector.

4 a domino iubemur.

5 miles gladio vulneratur.

6 a magistro laudamur.

7 a regina reguntur.

8 a militibus defendimini.

9 a domino punior.

10 a servis ducimur.

3 marks for each question. Total: 30

Exercise 1.14

Translate the following into English:

1 Sparta, urbs Graeca, a Menelao regitur. (6)

2 Helena, uxor Menelai, femina pulcherrima est. (6)

3 Helena tamen a Paride capitur. (5)

4 Helena ad urbem Troiam a Paride ducitur. (7)

5 Menelaus iratus est. (3)

6 multi milites a Menelao vocantur. (5)

7 multae naves a Graecis parantur. (5)

8 milites celeriter in naves ponuntur. (5)

9 mox naves trans mare ad urbem Troiam mittuntur. (8)

10 Troia a Graecis diu oppugnatur. (5)

Total: 55

Exercise 1.15

Translate the following into English:

1 multi viri fortissimi in bello occiduntur. (6)

2 Patroclus ab Hectore occiditur. (4)

3 Hector ab Achille occiditur. (4)

4 corpus Hectoris a civibus Troianis videtur. (6)

5 muri Troiae non delentur. (4)

6 urbs a Graecis non capitur. (5)

7 tandem equus maximus a Graecis aedificatur. (6)

8 equus prope urbem Troiam ponitur. (5)

9 miles a Graecis relinquitur. (4)

10 urbs Troia a Graecis tandem capitur. (6)

Total: 50

Exercise 1.16

Translate the following into Latin:

1 We are liked.

2 You (sing.) are being warned.

3 They are ruled.

4 I am heard.

5 You (pl.) are being conquered.

6 We are defended.

7 They are wounded.

8 He is being set free.

9 We are ordered.

10 They are being punished.

1 mark for each question. Total: 10

Exercise 1.17

Translate the following into Latin:

1 The slaves are being set free.

2 The pupil is being warned.

3 The city is being defended.

4 The walls are being destroyed.

5 Money is found.

2 marks for each question. Total: 10

Exercise 1.18

Translate the following into Latin:

1 The slave is set free by the master. (4)

2 The pupils are being punished by the teacher. (4)

3 The ship is being attacked by the soldiers. (4)

4 Fathers are often loved by their sons. (5)

5 Wars are not liked by women. (5)

6 Many towns are attacked by the Romans. (5)

7 That teacher is never liked by the pupils. (6)

8 Books are often read by wise boys. (6)

9 Helen is being led back by the Greeks. (4)

10 Good pupils are always praised by good teachers. (7)

Total: 50

Exercise 1.19

Translate these Latin verbs. Then, keeping the same person and number, change the verb from the active voice to the passive voice and translate your answer.

> **Example**
>
> amant   they love   amantur   they are loved

1 capitis.

2 audit.

3 video.

4 vulneramus.

5 defendis.

6 monemus.

7 oppugnatis.

8 punit.

9 iubes.

10 conspicit.

3 marks for each question. Total: 30

Exercise 1.20

Translate these Latin verbs. Then, keeping the same person and number, change the verb from the passive voice to the active voice and translate your answer.

> **Example**
>
> amatur   he is loved   amat   he loves

1 audimini.

2 oppugnamur.

3 ducuntur.

4 relinquuntur.

5 servaris.

6 vincitur.

7 vulneratur.

8 occidimur.

9 liberantur.

10 iubeor.

3 marks for each question. Total: 30

→ Revision

Exercise 1.21

Give and translate the following verb parts:

1 The 3rd person singular, present active of **moneo**.

2 The 3rd person singular, present passive of **moneo**.

3 The 1st person plural, perfect active of **convenio**.

4 The 2nd person singular, imperfect active of **reduco**.

5 The 3rd person plural, present active of **laudo**.

6 The 3rd person plural, present passive of **laudo**.

7 The 2nd person plural, future active of **sum**.

8 The 1st person singular, pluperfect active of **possum**.

9 The 3rd person plural, perfect active of **eo**.

10 The 2nd person singular, present passive of **vulnero**.

2 marks for each question. Total: 20

Exercise 1.22

Translate and give the person, number, tense, voice and 1st person singular of the present active of the following verbs:

1 convenient.

2 cucurrerunt.

3 dedit.

4 videntur.

5 laudamur.

6 conspicimini.

7 potuerunt.

8 posuerunt.

9 auditur.

10 fuerunt.

6 marks for each question. Total: 60

Exercise 1.23

Translate the following into English:

1 nolite me relinquere, amici! (4)

2 pauci senes in bellis pugnant. (5)

3 sunt multa templa in media urbe. (5)

4 nonne Flavia sapientior quam Marcus est? (6)

5 pauci iuvenes bene scribere possunt. (5)

Total: 25

Exercise 1.24

Translate the following into Latin:

1 The citizens praised the chieftains. (3)

2 The sad old men were running. (3)

3 We saw a big crowd. (3)

4 The brave soldiers make a long journey. (5)

5 The master frightens all the slaves with cruel words. (6)

Total: 20

Exercise 2.1

Translate the following passage. Line numbers are given on the left. New words are underlined in the text and their meanings given in the margin.

Ulysses (Odysseus) and the End of the War

1 urbs Troia a Graecis capta erat. Ulixes ipse
   laetissimus erat. ille enim erat qui Graecos equum
   ligneum aedificare iusserat. iam haec verba comitibus
   dixit: 'amici, gens Graeca felicissima est. nos a deis
5 amamur. nonne a nobis Troia capta est? a nobis muri
   deleti sunt; a nobis templa deleta sunt; paene omnes
   principes Troianorum a nobis interfecti sunt. multa
   pecunia a nobis capta est. multa praemia habemus.
   Helena, quae a Menelao magnopere amatur, ad
10 Graeciam nunc reducitur. credite mihi, amici! – mox
   omnes ad Graeciam redibimus! mox uxores nostras
   filiosque nostros filiasque nostras iterum videbimus!'

   diu tamen Ulixes uxorem suam, Penelopen nomine,
   non vidit. neque filium suum, Telemachum nomine,
15 vidit. multos annos cum comitibus trans maria erravit
   et maxima pericula subiit.

a/ab = by
capta erat = had been taken
ipse = himself
enim = for (giving an explanation)
qui = who
ligneus, -a, -um = wooden
gens, gentis, f. = race, tribe
capta est = has been taken
deleti, -a sunt = have been destroyed
paene = almost
interfecti sunt = have been killed
praemium, -ii, n. = prize, reward
quae = who
credo, -ere, credidi (3) + dative = I believe, trust
Penelopen = the accusative of Penelope (Greek form)
neque = nor, and … not
Telemachus, -i, m. = Telemachus
multos annos = for many years
subiit = (he) underwent

Total: 90

Exercise 2.2

1 From the passage give an example of:

   (a) a superlative adjective.   (1)

   (b) an adverb.   (1)

   (c) a verb in the future tense.   (1)

2 equum (line 2). In which case is this noun? Why is this case used?   (2)

3   iusserat (line 3). Give the person, number and tense of this verb.
Give the 1st person singular of the present active tense of this verb.   (4)

4   maria (line 15). Explain the connection between this Latin word and
the English word *marine*.   (1)

Total: 10

➜ Principal parts: a reminder

Example

1	2	3	4	5	6
amo	amare	amavi	amatum	(1)	I love

1   The 1st person singular of the present tense.
2   The present infinitive (to-word).
3   The 1st person singular of the perfect tense.
4   The supine. It is this which is used to form the perfect participle passive (PPP).
5   The verb conjugation number.
6   The English meaning of the verb.

Exercise 2.3

Give the past participle passive of each of the following verbs:

1   moneo, monere, monui, monitum (2), I warn.

2   rego, regere, rexi, rectum (3), I rule.

3   audio, audire, audivi, auditum (4), I hear.

4   porto, portare, portavi, portatum (1), I carry.

5   interficio, interficere, interfeci, interfectum (3½), I kill.

6   duco, ducere, duxi, ductum (3), I lead.

7   deleo, delere, delevi, deletum (2), I destroy.

8   capio, capere, cepi, captum (3½), I capture.

9   vulnero, vulnerare, vulneravi, vulneratum (1), I wound.

10 mitto, mittere, misi, missum (3), I send.

11 video, videre, vidi, visum (2), I see.

12 vinco, vincere, vici, victum (3), I conquer.

13 iacio, iacere, ieci, iactum (3½), I throw.

14 dico, dicere, dixi, dictum (3), I say.

15 punio, punire, punivi, punitum (4), I punish.

1 mark for each question. Total: 15

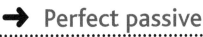

→ Perfect passive

Exercise 2.4

Translate the following into English:

1 interfectus est.
2 interfecta est.
3 interfecti sumus.
4 interfecti sunt.
5 vulnerata es.
6 missus sum.
7 capta est.
8 capti estis.
9 puniti sumus.
10 auditi sunt.

11 visus est.
12 visa est.
13 visi sunt.
14 portatae sumus.
15 victi sunt.
16 missus est.
17 missa est.
18 ducta est.
19 dictum est.
20 moniti estis.

2 marks for each question. Total: 40

Exercise 2.5

Translate the following into English:

1 puer punitus est.
2 pueri puniti sunt.
3 puella visa est.
4 puellae visae sunt.
5 templum aedificatum est.
6 templa aedificata sunt.
7 Romani victi sunt.
8 miles vulneratus est.
9 tela iacta sunt.
10 senex interfectus est.
11 oppidum oppugnatum est.
12 oppida oppugnata sunt.
13 discipuli moniti sunt.
14 discipulus monitus est.
15 pater amatus est.

16 mater amata est.

17 verba audita sunt.

18 voces auditae sunt.

19 urbs deleta est.

20 lux visa est.

3 marks for each question. Total: 60

Exercise 2.6

Translate the following into English:

1 dominus servum punivit. (3)

2 servus a domino punitus est. (5)

3 poeta librum misit. (3)

4 liber a poeta missus est. (5)

5 milites oppidum oppugnaverunt. (3)

6 oppidum a militibus oppugnatum est. (5)

7 Romani hostes interfecerunt. (3)

8 hostes a Romanis interfecti sunt. (5)

9 ego puellam vidi. (3)

10 puella a me visa est. (5)

Total: 40

Exercise 2.7

Translate the following into English:

1 rex multa verba dixit. (4)

2 multa verba a rege dicta sunt. (6)

3 puellae voces militum audiverunt. (4)

4 voces militum a puellis auditae sunt. (6)

5 servi mox cibum paraverunt. (4)

6 cibus a servis mox paratus est. (6)

7 Romani tandem Graecos vicerunt. (4)

8 Graeci a Romanis tandem victi sunt. (6)

9 puer puellam magnopere amavit. (4)

10 puella a puero magnopere amata est. (6)

Total: 50

Exercise 2.8

Translate the following into English:

1 Romani ab hostibus visi sunt. (5)

2 a domino punitus sum. (4)

3 puella a puero visa est. (5)

4 puellae a pueris visae sunt. (5)

5 templum a civibus aedificatum est. (5)

6 muri ab hostibus oppugnati sunt. (5)

7 multa verba a senibus dicta sunt. (6)

8 sagitta a milite iacta est. (5)

9 servus a domino liberatus est. (5)

10 donum a matre missum est. (5)

Total: 50

Exercise 2.9

Translate the following into English:

1 discipuli a magistro moniti sunt. (6)

2 servus a domino saevo punitus est. (5)

3 verba a me non audita sunt. (6)

4 clamor a magistro auditus est. (5)

5 ab hostibus visi sumus. (4)

6 a magistro laudatus es. (4)

7 multis sagittis vulneratus sum. (4)

8 oppidum a Romanis oppugnatum est. (5)

9 multi cives a militibus interfecti sunt. (6)

10 urbs a Graecis capta est. (5)

Total: 50

Exercise 2.10

Translate the following into Latin:

1 A book was written.

2 Presents were given.

3 The old man was killed.

4 The boys were ordered.

5 Wars were made.

6 Books were read.

7 The ship was moved.

8 The girl was ordered.

9 Help was given.

10 The sailor was killed.

3 marks for each question. Total: 30

Exercise 2.11

Translate the following into Latin:

1 Money was given by the master.

2 The books were written by the poet.

3 A messenger was sent by the king.

4 The book was read by the teacher.

5 The slaves have been killed by the master.

5 marks for each question. Total: 25

→ Revision

Exercise 2.12

Translate the following into Latin:

1 The general used to give big rewards. (4)

2 The Romans conquered many tribes. (4)

3 The daring slave killed the old man with his sword. (5)

4 Wise pupils read books. (4)

5 I am praising the brave soldier. (3)

Total: 20

Exercise 2.13

Put into the plural and translate your answer:

1 princeps tibi credit. (6)

2 clamorem audivi. (5)

3 magnum praemium militi dat. (8)

4 miles servum interfecit. (6)

5 servus a milite interfectus est. (10)

Total: 35

Exercise 2.14

Put into the singular and translate your answer:

1 senes currebant. (4)

2 gentes superantur. (4)

3 voces feminarum audivimus. (6)

4 servi mali puniti sunt. (8)

5 servi a dominis puniuntur. (8)

Total: 30

Exercise 2.15

Give the translation, person, number, tense, voice and 1st person singular of the present active of the following verbs:

1 interfecerunt.

2 credebat.

3 interfecta est.

4 bibisti.

5 clamabat.

6 defendunt.

7 defendent.

8 mansisti.

9 spectabamus.

10 portantur.

6 marks for each question. Total: 60

Exercise 2.16

Give and translate the following verb parts:

1 The 3rd person singular, perfect active of **amo**.

2 The 3rd person singular, perfect passive of **amo**.

3 The 3rd person plural, present active of **interficio**.

4 The 3rd person plural, present passive of **interficio**.

5 The 1st person singular, imperfect active of **credo**.

6 The 1st person plural, perfect active of **eo**.

7 The 2nd person plural, pluperfect active of **punio**.

8 The 3rd person singular, perfect active of **curro**.

9 The 3rd person plural, imperfect active of **video**.

10 The 2nd person singular, perfect active of **conspicio**.

2 marks for each question. Total: 20

Exercise 2.17

Translate the following into English:

1 discipuli a magistris non saepe laudantur. (6)

2 ex urbe cras discedemus. (4)

3 omnes servi magnos gladios tenebant. (5)

4 a domino crudeli saepe punimur. (5)

5 num hoc donum optimum est? (5)

Total: 25

3

Translate the following passage. Line numbers are given on the left. New words are underlined in the text and their meanings given in the margin.

Odysseus reaches the land of the Lotus-eaters

1 post decem <u>annos tota</u> urbs Troia a Graecis <u>capta</u>
<u>erat</u>. muri <u>deleti erant</u> et templa <u>incensa erant</u>,
neque multi Troiani effugere potuerant. <u>Ulixes</u>
comitesque Troia discesserant et ad Graeciam
5 navibus redibant. multos <u>dies</u> trans mare
navigaverunt. tandem naves Graecorum ad terram
<u>Lotophagorum tempestate pulsae sunt</u>. ei <u>qui lotum</u>
consumunt semper dormire et in hac terra manere
<u>volunt</u>.

10 <u>Ulixes</u> tres nautas ad oppidum <u>Lotophagorum</u> misit.
hos nautas cibum aquamque <u>petere</u> et ad naves
quattuor aut quinque <u>horis</u> redire iussit. <u>ipse interea</u>
cum ceteris comitibus prope naves mansit. multas
<u>horas</u> ibi manserunt. post septem <u>horas</u> tamen tres
15 nautae non redierant. a <u>Lotophagis tenebantur</u>. <u>res</u>
<u>Ulixem</u> terrebat. <u>sollicitus</u> erat.

annus, -i, m. = year
totus, -a, -um = whole
capta erat = had been taken
deleti erant = had been destroyed
incensa erant = had been burned
Ulixes = Ulysses/Odysseus
dies = days
Lotophagi, -orum, m. pl. = Lotus Eaters
tempestas, tempestatis, f. = storm
pello, -ere, pepuli, pulsum (3) = I drive
qui = who
lotus, -i, f. = the fruit of the lotus
volunt = (they) want
peto, -ere, petivi, petitum (3) = I look for
hora, -ae, f. = hour
ipse = he himself
interea = meanwhile
tenebantur = they were being held
res = the situation
sollicitus, -a, -um = worried

Total: 80

1 From the passage give an example of:

(a) a cardinal number. (1)

(b) an infinitive. (1)

(c) a preposition. (1)

2 discesserant (line 4). In which tense is this verb? Give the 1st person singular of the present tense of this verb. (2)

3 mare (line 5). In which case is this noun? Why is this case used? (2)

4 dormire (line 8). What does this word mean? Explain the connection between dormire and the English word *dormitory*. (2)

5 nautas (line 11). What is the gender of this noun? (1)

Total: 10

→ Pluperfect passive

Exercise 3.3

Translate the following into English:

1 visi eramus.

2 motum erat.

3 laudata erat.

4 necati erant.

5 ducti eramus.

6 captus eras.

7 missus eram.

8 captus erat.

9 capta erat.

10 vulnerati eramus.

11 datum erat.

12 scriptum erat.

13 deletum erat.

14 rogatus eras.

15 ductus erat.

16 puniti eratis.

17 iussi eramus.

18 visa erat.

19 nuntiatum erat.

20 occisus erat.

2 marks for each question. Total: 40

Exercise 3.4

Translate the following into English:

1 tandem copiae paratae erant. (4)

2 hastis vulneratus erat. (3)

3 hastis vulnerata erat. (3)

4 a magistro laudati eramus. (4)

5 omnes muri ab hostibus deleti erant. (6)

6 ab amicis relictus eram. (4)

7 a Romanis superati eratis. (4)

8 a magistro auditi eramus. (4)

9 a Graecis victi erant. (4)

10 a domino liberatus eras. (4)

Total: 40

Exercise 3.5

Translate the following into English:

1 Helena a Paride capta erat. (5)

2 Helena ad urbem Troiam ducta erat. (6)

3 naves a Graecis paratae erant. (5)

4 naves ad urbem Troiam missae erant. (6)

5 Troia a Graecis oppugnata erat. (5)

6 multi viri occisi erant. (4)

7 equus maximus a Graecis aedificatus erat. (6)

8 equus in media urbe a Troianis positus erat. (8)

9 multi Troiani a Graecis interfecti erant. (6)

10 urbs tandem capta erat. (4)

Total: 55

Exercise 3.6

Translate the following into Latin:

1 The book had been written.

2 The pupil had been punished.

3 The boys had been warned.

4 The girl had been seen.

5 The soldier had been wounded.

6 The ship had been built.

7 The weapons had been collected.

8 The woman had been saved.

9 The soldiers had been killed.

10 The temple had been destroyed.

3 marks for each question. Total: 30

Exercise 3.7

Translate the following into Latin:

1 The girl had been led back by the Greeks.

2 The slaves had been set free by the master.

3 The wall had been built by slaves.

4 Dinner had been prepared by the maidservant.

5 The Greeks had been conquered by the Romans.

5 marks for each question. Total: 25

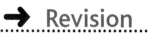

→ Revision

Exercise 3.8

Translate the following into Latin:

1 A great storm destroyed the ship. (4)

2 The wind drove the ships. (3)

3 The soldiers received many rewards. (4)

4 All boys like beautiful girls. (5)

5 We are seeking food and water. (4)

Total: 20

Exercise 3.9

Translate the following into Latin:

1 Many men were running. (3)

2 All teachers are wise. (4)

3 The evil slave was escaping. (3)

4 The citizens fled. (2)

5 Many ships are approaching. (3)

Total: 15

Exercise 3.10

Translate the following into Latin:

1 The great storm destroyed the ship. (4)

2 The shouts frightened the old man. (3)

3 The teacher had a very loud (big) voice. (5)

4 The soldiers soon seized the city. (4)

5 All horses like food. (4)

Total: 20

Exercise 3.11

Translate the following into Latin:

1 I have a famous brother. (3)

2 All the companions feared death. (4)

3 The brave citizens were defending the town. (4)

4 The king announced a difficult task. (4)

5 We saw a bright light on the journey. (5)

Total: 20

Exercise 3.12

Translate the following into Latin:

1   The soldier received many wounds in the battle.   (6)
2   The Roman chieftains met in the city.   (5)
3   The daring slaves were running out of the town.   (5)
4   The cruel master killed the sad old man.   (5)
5   The wretched young men departed without delay.   (4)

Total: 25

Exercise 3.13

Translate the following into English:

1   tempestates naves saepe delent.   (4)
2   discipuli sapientes magistris numquam credunt.   (5)
3   Romani multas gentes vicerunt.   (4)
4   domini crudeles a servis numquam amantur.   (6)
5   multi servi iam ex oppido effugerant.   (6)

Total: 25

Exercise 3.14

Translate the following into English:

1   noli illum bonum servum punire, domine!   (6)
2   num omnes naves in illa tempestate deletae sunt?   (8)
3   senes sapientissimi hoc facere numquam poterunt.   (6)
4   iuvenes magna praemia saepe petunt.   (5)
5   Romani igitur totam urbem deleverunt.   (5)

Total: 30

Exercise 3.15

Translate the following into English:

1   dux virtutem omnium civium laudavit.   (5)
2   magister multa dona discipulis sapientibus dedit.   (6)
3   ille malus servus ab hoc domino cras monebitur.   (8)
4   pauci senes sapientes sunt.   (4)
5   nautae tempestatem saeviorem quam illam numquam viderant.   (7)

Total: 30

Exercise 3.16

Translate the following into English:

1 auxilio Romanorum totam urbem mox occupabimus.   (6)

2 multi Graecorum in illo proelio interfecti sunt.   (7)

3 plurimi cives prope templum Iovis convenerunt.   (6)

4 pauci senes in urbe relicti erant.   (6)

5 nemo sapientior est quam ego.   (5)

Total: 30

Exercise 3.17

Keeping the same person, number and voice, put each of the following into the perfect tense, then translate your answer:

1 pello.

2 interficiunt.

3 convenitis.

4 ducis.

5 potest.

2 marks for each question. Total: 10

Exercise 3.18

Give and translate the following verb parts:

1 The 3rd person singular, present passive of porto.

2 The 1st person plural, present active of video.

3 The 2nd person singular, imperfect active of mitto.

4 The 3rd person plural, perfect passive of duco.

5 The 3rd person singular, perfect active of curro.

6 The 1st person singular, perfect active of scribo.

7 The 2nd person plural, imperfect active of sum.

8 The 3rd person singular, imperfect active of iacio.

9 The 1st person plural, present active of vinco.

10 The 3rd person plural, imperfect active of appropinquo.

2 marks for each question. Total: 20

Exercise 3.19

Translate these verbs into English. Then give the person, number, tense, voice (active or passive) and the 1st person singular of the present active of each verb.

Example

| amavit | he loved | 3rd person | Singular | Perfect | Active | amo |

1 electus es.

2 scripserunt.

3 conspexit.

4 liberamur.

5 iit.

6 poterant.

7 victus est.

8 festinabamus.

9 adveniemus.

10 fuerunt.

6 marks for each question. Total: 60

Exercise 3.20

Put the following into the plural and translate your answer:

1 urbs oppugnata est.

2 liber legitur.

3 servus liberatus erat.

4 oppidum defenditur.

5 senex interfectus est.

6 marks for each question. Total: 30

Exercise 3.21

Put the following into the singular and translate your answer:

1 pueri puniti sunt.

2 senes relinquuntur.

3 naves paratae erant.

4 milites vulnerantur.

5 feminae spectantur.

6 marks for each question. Total: 30

Exercise 3.22

Translate the following into English:

1 plurimae naves a Romanis aedificatae sunt. (7)

2 donum patri meo cras dabo. (5)

3 veniesne mecum? (4)

4 librum bonum heri legi. (4)

5 hic liber longissimus erat. (5)

Total: 25

Exercise 4.1

Translate the following passage. Line numbers are given on the left. New words are underlined in the text and their meanings given in the margin.

Odysseus finds his three missing sailors

1 Ulixes comitesque multas horas prope naves manserunt. tres nautae, <u>qui</u> ad <u>Lotophagos</u> missi erant, non redierant. tandem Ulixes <u>sollicitus</u> nautas petere constituit. haec verba comitibus dixit:

5 '<u>sollicitus</u> sum. amici nostri non redierunt. diu absunt. <u>fortasse</u> a <u>Lotophagis</u> tenentur. ego eos petere <u>volo</u>. quis mecum venire <u>vult</u>?'

comites inter se spectabant. deinde clamaverunt: 'hic manere <u>nolumus</u>. omnes tecum ire <u>volumus</u>. amici
10 nostri a nobis mox <u>liberabuntur</u>.' Ulixes, ubi haec verba audivit, laetus erat. paucos comites prope naves reliquit <u>atque</u> illis 'naves bene <u>custodite</u>!' inquit. 'ego ceterique paucis horis redibimus. nautas mox inveniemus.'

15 Ulixes comitesque ad oppidum <u>Lotophagorum</u> <u>contenderunt</u>. nautas, <u>qui</u> a <u>Lotophagis</u> tenebantur, mox invenerunt. sed ubi eos viderunt, <u>attoniti</u> erant.

qui = who
Lotophagi, -orum, m.
pl. = Lotus Eaters
sollicitus, -a, -um =
worried
fortasse = perhaps
volo = I want

vult = wants
nolumus = we do not
want

volumus = we want
liberabuntur = will be
set free
atque = and
custodes = as guards
custodio, -ire,
custodivi, custoditum
(4) = I guard
contendo, -ere,
contendi (3) = I march,
I hurry
tenebantur = were
being held
attonitus, -a, -um =
amazed

Total: 95

Exercise 4.2

1 From the passage give an example of:

　(a) a verb in the pluperfect passive. (1)

　(b) an adverb. (1)

　(c) an imperative. (1)

　(d) a verb in the future tense. (1)

2 verba (line 4). Give the gender of this noun. (1)

3 absunt (line 6). Give the person and number of this verb. Give the 1st person singular of the present tense of this verb. (3)

4 naves (line 12). In which case is this noun? Why is this case used? (2)

Total: 10

Exercise 4.3

Translate the following into English:

1 volumus.		11 noles.	
2 non vult.		12 velle.	
3 volebat.		13 volent.	
4 volebant.		14 noluit.	
5 nolebat.		15 volebatis.	
6 nolebant.		16 non vis.	
7 non vultis.		17 nolle.	
8 voluit.		18 nolunt.	
9 voluerunt.		19 volet.	
10 vis.		20 noluerunt.	

1 mark for each question. Total: 20

Exercise 4.4

Translate the following into English:

1 manere noluerunt. (2)

2 discedere voluerunt. (2)

3 visne mecum ire? (4)

4 effugere nolumus. (2)

5 ridere volebam. (2)

6 sapiens esse vult. (3)

7 hoc facere non vult. (4)

8 laborare nolo. (2)

9 ludere volo. (2)

10 cantare nolebat. (2)

Total: 25

Exercise 4.5

Translate the following into English:

1 Graeci Troiam oppugnare volebant. (4)

2 hi discipuli laborare numquam volunt. (5)

3 Ulixes ad Graeciam redire volebat. (5)

4 hic puer laborare non vult. (5)

5 milites autem hoc facere nolebant. (5)

6 puer magistrum audire nolebat. (4)

7 Helena ad urbem Troiam ire nolebat. (6)

8 omnes discipuli sapientes esse volunt. (5)

9 Romani multas gentes vincere volebant. (5)

10 magister bonus discipulos terrere non vult. (6)

Total: 50

→ Time

Expressions of time in Latin have either accusative or ablative endings. Time 'how long?' is expressed by the accusative. Time 'when?' is expressed by the ablative.

accusative endings	ablative endings
multos annos	secundo anno
for many years	in the second year
tres horas	tertia hora
for three hours	at the third hour
quattuor dies	quarto die
for four days	on the fourth day
totam noctem	quinque annis
for the whole night	within five years

Exercise 4.6

Translate the following into English:

1 multos annos.

2 paucas horas.

3 multos dies.

4 paucos dies.

5 quinque horas.

6 totum diem.

7 multas horas.

8 duas horas.

9 tres dies.

10 sex annos.

2 marks for each question. Total: 20

Exercise 4.7

Translate the following into English:

1 paucis horis.

2 tertio die.

3 decima hora.

4 illo tempore.

5 quarto die.

6 illa* die.

7 octo diebus.

8 paucis diebus.

9 quattuor annis.

10 sexto anno.

* feminine as it refers to a specific day

2 marks for each question. Total: 20

Exercise 4.8

Translate the following into English:

1 paucis diebus veniam. (3)

2 totum diem dormivi. (3)

3 multas horas currebam; nunc fessus sum. (6)

4 paucis annis redibo. (3)

5 septem dies laboravimus. (3)

6 quarto anno advenerunt. (3)

7 paucis horis discedemus. (3)

8 eum tertia hora vidi. (4)

9 multas horas non dormivit. (4)

10 multos dies laborabo. (3)

Total: 35

Exercise 4.9

Translate the following into English:

1 multae naves a Graecis paucis diebus paratae sunt. (8)

2 nautae trans mare multos dies navigaverunt. (6)

3 Graeci Troiam multos annos oppugnaverunt. (5)

4 tandem Graeci Troiam decimo anno ceperunt. (6)

5 Troiani contra Graecos multas horas pugnaverunt. (6)

6 muri paucis horis deleti sunt. (5)

7 omnes Graeci quinque diebus discesserunt. (5)

8 Ulixes trans mare multos annos erravit. (6)

9 Ulixes nautas paucis horis redire iussit. (6)

10 nautae cum Lotophagis multos dies manere cupiebant. (7)

Total: 60

Exercise 4.10

Translate the following into Latin:

1 I want to work. (2)

2 I do not want to play. (2)

3 We want to laugh. (2)

4 They wanted to sing. (2)

5 I wanted to escape. (2)

6 No one wants to work. (3)

7 We did not want to come today. (3)

8 Sextus, you want to hurry. (3)

9 Do you (sing.) want to hurry? (3)

10 He wants to sleep now. (3)

Total: 25

Exercise 4.11

Translate the following into Latin:

1 Slaves always want to escape.

2 The pupils did not want to work yesterday.

3 That boy will not want to do this.

4 The soldiers wanted to fight well.

5 Old men do not often want to run.

4 marks for each question. Total: 20

Exercise 4.12

Translate the following into Latin:

1 The citizens wanted to defend their city well.

2 The good master wants to guard his slaves.

3 Few pupils want to work well.

4 The enemy wanted to attack the walls immediately.

5 The slaves will want to kill their cruel master.

5 marks for each question. Total: 25

→ Revision

Exercise 4.13

Give and translate the following verb parts:

1 The 3rd person singular, present active of volo.

2 The 3rd person plural, present passive of custodio.

3 The 3rd person plural, perfect active of mitto.

4 The 3rd person plural, perfect passive of mitto.

5 The 2nd person singular, present active of **volo**.

6 The 1st person plural, perfect active of **contendo**.

7 The 2nd person singular, imperfect active of **eo**.

8 The 3rd person singular, imperfect active of **possum**.

9 The 2nd person plural, pluperfect active of **curro**.

10 The 3rd person plural, perfect active of **sum**.

2 marks for each question. Total: 20

Exercise 4.14

Give the translation, person, number, tense, voice and 1st person singular of the present active of the following verbs:

1 interficitur.

2 contenderunt.

3 pulsus est.

4 discedam.

5 ierunt.

6 pepulerunt.

7 volebat.

8 visus erat.

9 stetit.

10 mansimus.

6 marks for each question. Total: 60

Exercise 4.15

Put into the singular and translate your answer:

1 laborare nolumus. (1 + 2)

2 custodes servos necabant. (3 + 3)

3 oppida a militibus occupata sunt. (4 + 5)

4 milites bene pugnaverunt. (2 + 3)

5 praemia militibus saepe dantur. (3 + 4)

Total: 30

Exercise 4.16

Put into the plural and translate your answer:

1 miles contendebat. (2 + 2)

2 malum custodem non amo. (3 + 4)

3 opus difficile numquam facio. (3 + 4)

4 haec gens superata est. (4 + 4)

5 tempestas navem ad insulam pepulit. (4 + 5)

Total: 35

Exercise 4.17

Translate the following into Latin:

1 I will work for many days.

2 I slept all night.

3 We will come within four days.

4 He arrived at the second hour.

5 They came on the fourth day.

3 marks for each question. Total: 15

Exercise 4.18

Translate the following into Latin:

1 The Greeks attacked the city for nine years.   (5)

2 In the tenth year the city was captured by the Greeks.   (6)

3 The messenger caught sight of the city on the fourth day.   (5)

4 Ulixes stayed on the island for many days.   (6)

5 That night I saw many beautiful girls in the town.   (8)

Total: 30

Exercise 4.19

Translate the following into English:

1 templum deis aedificamus.   (4)

2 filium et filiam habeo. eos amo.   (8)

3 dux nuntium ad hostes mittere constituit.   (6)

4 auxilio sociorum urbem occupavimus.   (5)

5 quod sapiens sum, omnia scio.   (7)

Total: 30

Exercise 4.20

Translate the following into Latin:

1 A slave was guarding the noble citizens.   (4)

2 The old men were defending the town with their long swords.   (5)

3 Wise slaves do not kill their masters.   (5)

4 We have seen the guard.   (2)

5 My wife loves villas.   (4)

Total: 20

Exercise 5.1

Translate the following passage. Line numbers are given on the left. New words are underlined in the text and their meanings given in the margin.

Odysseus deals with his three missing sailors

1 Ulixes, nautas <u>petens</u>, ad oppidum
   <u>Lotophagorum</u> advenerat. nautae a <u>Lotophagis</u>
   <u>tenebantur</u>. Ulixes, ubi eos vidit, <u>attonitus</u> erat.
   illi <u>enim</u> <u>semisomni</u> erant neque se movere
5 volebant.

   'quid facitis?' eos rogavit Ulixes iratus. 'quid
   fecistis?'

   nautae ei responderunt: 'noli iratus esse,
   Ulixes. <u>lotum</u> consumpsimus. <u>lotus</u> optima est.
10 eam amamus. hic manere et dormire volumus.
   <u>domum</u> ire nolumus. nos hic relinque!'

   Ulixes autem hoc facere nolebat. nautis igitur
   'hoc facere nolo,' inquit. 'ad naves statim
   <u>feremini</u>.' deinde comitibus clamavit: '<u>ferte</u>
15 <u>funes</u>! hos nautas <u>funibus</u> <u>vincite</u>! deinde eos
   ad naves <u>ferte</u>!' comites Ulixis ea <u>quae</u> iusserat
   fecerunt. nautas <u>funibus</u> <u>vinxerunt</u>. nautae, his
   <u>funibus</u> <u>vincti</u>, magna voce <u>clamantes</u>, ad
   naves <u>lati sunt</u>.

petens = looking for
Lotophagi, -orum, m. pl. =
Lotus Eaters
tenebantur = (they) were
being held
attonitus, -a, -um = amazed
enim = for
semisomni = half asleep

lotus, -i, f. = the lotus fruit

domum = home

feremini = you will be carried
fero, ferre, tuli, latum (irreg.)
= I bring, I carry
funis, -is, m. = rope
vincio, -ire, vinxi, vinctum
(3) = I tie up
quae = which (the things
which)
vincti = tied up
clamantes = shouting
lati sunt = *see* fero *above*

Total: 85

Exercise 5.2

1 From the passage give an example of:

   (a) a verb in the pluperfect tense.   (1)

   (b) an infinitive.   (1)

   (c) an imperative.   (1)

2 eos (line 3). Give the nominative masculine singular of this pronoun. (1)

3 Ulixes (line 6). In which case is this noun?   (1)

4 optima (line 9). This is a superlative adjective. Give the nominative masculine singular of the positive form of this adjective. (1)

5 naves (line 13). In which case is this noun? Why is this case used? (2)

6 iusserat (line 16). Give the 1st person singular of the present tense of this verb. (1)

7 Using your knowledge of Latin and a clue from the passage above, work out what a *funambulist* does. (1)

Total: 10

→ fero, ferre, tuli, latum = I bear, I carry

Exercise 5.3

Translate the following into English:

1 fers.

2 feretur.

3 tulit.

4 ferre.

5 tuli.

6 tulerunt.

7 lati sunt.

8 latus est.

9 fert.

10 feremus.

11 ferebat.

12 ferebatur.

13 ferent.

14 ferunt.

15 tuleramus.

1 mark for each question. Total: 15

Exercise 5.4

Translate the following into English:

1 servus multum cibum tulerat. (4)

2 multam pecuniam cras feram. (4)

3 quid fers? (2)

4 milites arma ferunt. (3)

5 arma a servis ferebantur. (4)

6 quid a servis cras feretur? (5)

7 cibus in villam a servis cras feretur. (7)

8 gladii a militibus lati sunt. (5)

9 quid servus ferebat? (3)

10 servus corpus ferebat. (3)

Total: 40

→ Revision

Exercise 5.5

Translate the following into English:

1 portabantur.

2 missi sunt.

3 audiar.

4 vulneratus sum.

5 regebamur.

6 occisi erant.

7 timebor.

8 punitus sum.

9 conspecti eramus.

10 interfecti sunt.

11 capiemur.

12 non vincar.

13 iubebamur.

14 feremur.

15 ducti estis.

16 mitteris.

17 missi erant.

18 ponitur.

19 occisus est.

20 occisa est.

21 legebatur.

22 vocatus sum.

23 vocabor.

24 laudatus sum.

25 laudor.

26 deletus est.

27 necati sunt.

28 parabantur.

29 moti sunt.

30 movemur.

31 oppugnati eramus.

32 datum est.

33 nuntiatum est.

34 visi sunt.

35 dicetur.

36 puniebantur.

37 victi sumus.

38 audiuntur.

39 puniemur.

40 laudamur.

1 mark for each question. Total: 40

Exercise 5.6

Translate the following into English:

1 multae hastae a militibus in proelio iactae sunt. (8)

2 templa urbis mox ab hostibus delebuntur. (6)

3 nuntii nostri ab hostibus capti sunt. (6)

4 pecunia militibus a duce data est. (6)

5 pecunia a militibus laetis accepta est. (6)

6 pecunia amici seni data est. (5)

7 multae terrae a regina reguntur. (5)

8 multi servi per vias ducebantur. (5)

9 oppidum ab hostibus iam deletum erat. (6)

10 ille dux a multis militibus non amatur. (7)

Total: 60

Exercise 5.7

Translate the following into English:

1 rex a fratre occisus est. (5)

2 pueri a patribus saepe monentur. (5)

3 multa praemia servis data sunt. (5)

4 iter longum a militibus factum erat. (6)

5 multae puellae pulchrae in via a pueris visae sunt. (9)

6 Romani ab hostibus numquam vincentur. (5)

7 haec urbs ab hostibus oppugnata est. (6)

8 multi milites ad urbem Troiam missi sunt. (7)

9 pueri ab illo magistro saepe puniuntur. (6)

10 multi milites in bello occisi sunt. (6)

Total: 60

Exercise 5.8

Translate the following into English:

1 magister a pueris non amatur. (5)

2 miles gladio vulneratus est. (4)

3 multus cibus in flumen a servis iacitur. (7)

4 ab hostibus oppugnamur! (3)

5 multa vulnera a militibus accepta erant. (6)

6 hic servus a domino cras punietur. (6)

7 multa verba a duce dicta sunt. (6)

8 pecunia civibus a rege data est. (6)

9 arma hostium a Romanis capta sunt. (6)

10 femina pulchra a puero conspecta est. (6)

Total: 55

Exercise 5.9

Translate the following into English:

1 quis a magistro cras laudabitur? (5)

2 multi discipuli a magistro cras laudabuntur. (6)

3 multi equi ex agris ducebantur. (5)

4 numquam a Romanis superabimur. (4)

5 nuntius ad urbem missus est. (5)

6 pueri ab illo magistro saepe puniuntur. (6)

7 multae naves a Graecis paratae erant. (6)

8 hic liber a me mox legetur. (6)

9 multa arma militibus a duce data sunt. (7)

10 laudaris quod fortis es, puer! (5)

Total: 55

Exercise 5.10

Translate the following into English:

1 ego ab omnibus puellis amor. (5)

2 templum magnum in hoc monte aedificabitur. (6)

3 multi hostes a Romanis victi sunt. (6)

4 dominus a servis timetur quod crudelis est. (7)

5 multi Romani sagittis vulnerati sunt. (5)

6 cena bona a matre parabitur. (5)

7 puer malus a magistro punitus erat. (6)

8 pecunia in via a puero inventa est. (7)

9 multae viae longae a Romanis aedificatae sunt. (7)

10 urbs Troia a Graecis oppugnata est. (6)

Total: 60

Exercise 5.11

Translate the following into English:

1 post decem annos urbs Troia capta est. (7)

2 verba longa a pueris parvis non saepe dicuntur. (8)

3 Graeci in Britannia non saepe videntur. (6)

4 multa verba a magistris saepe dicuntur. (6)

5 hoc periculum a servis non visum est. (7)

6 multi agri ab hostibus delebantur. (5)

7 ille equus vulneratus a milite hasta necatus est. (8)

8 multae gentes a Romanis superatae sunt. (6)

9 Graeci a Romanis tandem victi sunt. (6)

10 multa tela a servis facta erant. (6)

Total: 65

Exercise 5.12

Translate the following into Latin:

1 The young men were shouting in a loud voice. (4)

2 I have a famous brother and a beautiful sister. (6)

3 The enemy were approaching. (2)

4 The cruel master punished all the slaves. (5)

5 The queen likes money. (3)

Total: 20

Exercise 5.13

Translate the following into Latin:

1 You (sing.) are carried.

2 To carry.

3 He was carried.

4 She was carried.

5 We will be carried.

6 You (plural) will carry.

7 We had carried.

8 She is carrying.

9 She is being carried.

10 They were being carried.

1 mark for each question. Total: 10

Exercise 5.14

Translate the following into Latin:

1 The slave is carrying food and water. (5)

2 The soldiers were carrying swords and shields. (5)

3 Food was being carried into the villa by the slaves. (6)

4 Weapons were being carried by the soldiers. (4)

5 Bring money and food, slave! (5)

Total: 25

Exercise 5.15

Put into the plural and translate your answer:

1 saepe laudor.   (1 + 2)

2 civis reginam amat.   (3 + 3)

3 puer puellam forte conspexit.   (3 + 4)

4 puella amabatur.   (2 + 2)

5 urbs mox occupabitur.   (2 + 3)

Total: 25

Exercise 5.16

Put into the singular and translate your answer:

1 custodiebamur.   (1 + 1)

2 milites duces laudant.   (3 + 3)

3 servi punientur.   (2 + 2)

4 milites urbes ceperunt.   (3 + 3)

5 gladii a servis ferebantur.   (3 + 4)

Total: 25

Exercise 5.17

Give the translation, person, number, tense, voice and 1st person singular of the present active of the following verbs.

1 latus est.   6 tulerunt.

2 ii.   7 fuit.

3 erat.   8 ibat.

4 vulneraverat.   9 punitur.

5 iussit.   10 scripsisti.

6 marks for each question. Total: 60

Exercise 5.18

Give and translate the following verb parts:

1 The 2nd person plural, present active of **audio**.

2 The 3rd person plural, perfect active of **discedo**.

3 The 1st person singular, perfect active of **sum**.

4 The 3rd person singular, imperfect active of **sum**.

5 The 3rd person plural, imperfect active of **canto**.

6 The 1st person plural, present passive of **vulnero**.

7 The 3rd person singular, imperfect passive of **punio**.

8 The 3rd person plural, imperfect passive of **oppugno**.

9 The 2nd person singular, future passive of **mitto**.

10 The 3rd person plural, perfect passive of **occido**.

2 marks for each question. Total: 20

Exercise 5.19

Translate the following into Latin:

1 We will all be killed.

2 The city will be captured.

3 The girl was being watched.

4 Swords were being carried.

5 The walls will be attacked.

6 Food was being eaten.

7 The Romans will be beaten.

8 Money was being collected.

9 The cities will be defended.

10 Everything will be prepared.

2 marks for each question. Total: 20

Exercise 5.20

Translate the following into English:

1 illam puellam specta! eam amo!

2 hic puer patrem clarum habet.

3 illa tempestas multas naves delevit.

4 Flavia pulcherrima omnium puellarum est.

5 nolite timere, cives! auxilium adveniet.

5 marks for each question. Total: 25

Exercise 5.21

Translate the following into Latin:

1 I was always liked by that teacher.

2 Food was being prepared by those maidservants.

3 The beautiful girls will be watched by the boys.

4 The ship was being driven quickly towards the island.

5 These slaves will be punished by the master.

5 marks for each question. Total: 25

6

Exercise 6.1

Translate the following passage. Line numbers are given on the left. New words are underlined in the text and their meanings given in the margin.

Odysseus and his men leave the land of the Lotus-eaters

1 nautae qui lotum consumpserant, magna voce
clamantes, ex oppido Lotophagorum ad naves
a comitibus ferebantur. ei qui naves
custodiebant, ubi hos appropinquantes
5 viderunt, laetissimi erant. Ulixes ipse, in litore
stans, custodibus clamavit:

'hi nautae in hac terra a Lotophagis manere
cogebantur. lotum consumpserunt. domum ire
nolunt. eos in naves iacite! celeriter discedite!'

10 Graeci, ubi nautas in naves iecerunt, omnia
celeriter paraverunt. hoc labore facto, in
navibus – quae celerrimae erant – e terra
Lotophagorum discedere poterant.

qui = who
lotus, -i, f. = the lotus fruit
clamantes = shouting
Lotophagi, -orum, m. pl. =
the Lotus Eaters
appropinquantes =
approaching
ipse = himself
litus, -oris, n. = beach
stans = standing
cogo, -ere, coegi, coactum
(3) = I force

labor, -oris, m, = task
facto = having been done
quae = which
celer, celeris, celere = quick
(celerrimae *is superlative*)

Total: 55

Exercise 6.2

1 From the passage give an example of:

(a) a verb in the passive. (1)

(b) an infinitive. (1)

(c) an imperative. (1)

2 consumpserant (line 1). Give the person, number and tense of this verb.

Give the 1st person singular of the present tense of this verb. (4)

3 oppido (line 2). In which case is this noun? Why is this case used? (2)

4 laetissimi (line 5). This is a superlative adjective. Give the nominative masculine singular of the positive form of this adjective. (1)

Total: 10

→ Relative clauses in Latin: a reminder

In Latin the relative pronoun agrees with its antecedent in gender (masculine, feminine, neuter) and number (singular, plural). Its case is decided by its function in the relative clause.

> **Examples**
>
> puella, **quae** per viam ambulat, pulchra est.
> The girl, **who** is walking along the road, is beautiful.
>
> puella, **quam** specto, pulchra est.
> The girl, **whom** I am watching, is beautiful.
>
> puella, **cuius** pater dux est, dives est.
> The girl, **whose** father is a general, is wealthy.
>
> puella, **cui** librum dedi, semper legit.
> The girl, **to whom** I gave the book, is always reading.

Exercise 6.3

Translate the following into English:

1 hic est servus qui bene laborat.	(6)
2 haec est ancilla quae bene laborat.	(6)
3 hoc est templum quod maximum est.	(6)
4 hi sunt servi qui heri fugerunt.	(6)
5 hae sunt puellae quae bene cantant.	(6)
6 ille magister est quem non amo.	(6)
7 illa puella pulchra est quam amo.	(6)
8 hoc vinum est quod saepe bibo.	(6)
9 illi servi sunt quos dominus saepe punit.	(7)
10 hastae quas fero longae sunt.	(5)

Total: 60

Exercise 6.4

Translate the following into English:

1 hic est servus bonus cui pecuniam dedi.	(7)
2 hi sunt servi quibus pecuniam dedi.	(6)
3 haec est puella cuius pater clarus est.	(7)
4 hi sunt servi quorum dominus crudelis est.	(7)
5 villa in qua habito parva est.	(6)
6 hi sunt pueri quibuscum saepe ludo.	(6)
7 puer quocum ludo amicus meus est.	(6)

8 verba quae dixit magister mala erant. (6)

9 ibi est villa ex qua multi servi effugerunt. (8)

10 femina alta quam vides perterrita est. (6)

Total: 65

Exercise 6.5

Translate the following into English:

1 Menelaus, cuius uxor Helena erat, clarissimus erat. (7)

2 Paris, qui princeps Troianus erat, ad Menelaum venit. (8)

3 Paris Helenam, quae pulcherrima erat, capere constituit. (7)

4 Paris Helenam ad urbem Troiam in nave, quae celerrima erat, duxit. (11)

5 Menelaus, qui iratissimus erat, nuntios ad omnes urbes Graeciae misit. (10)

6 copiae quas Menelaus collegit magnae erant. (6)

7 Troia erat oppidum cuius muri validi erant. (7)

8 Menelaus Troiam, quae magna urbs erat, delere cupiebat. (8)

9 milites quos laudavit Menelaus fortissimi erant. (6)

10 Helena, quam Menelaus magnopere amabat, ad Graeciam tandem reducta est. (10)

Graecia, -ae, f. = Greece

Total: 80

→ Present participles

Present participles must agree with the person doing the action. They are easily spotted in Latin by the -ns or -nt after the stem.

Examples

1 miles pro patria **pugnans** occisus est.

The soldier was killed
{ fighting
whilst fighting
as he was fighting }
for his country.

2 pueri magistrum **appropinquantem** viderunt.

The boys saw the master
{ approaching.
as he was approaching.
while he was approaching. }

3 feminas **clamantes** audivimus.

We heard women shouting.

4 turbam feminarum **clamantium** audivimus.

We heard a crowd of shouting women.

41

> **Reminder:** the irregular present participle of **eo, ire, ii, itum** (I go) is: **iens, euntis** (going).

Exercise 6.6

Translate the following into English:

1 servi dominum appropinquantem mox viderunt. (5)

2 nautae clamantes ad navem ferebantur. (5)

3 feminas flentes videre numquam volumus. (5)

4 senes in templo sedentes vidimus. (5)

5 milites fortiter pugnantes interfecti sunt. (5)

6 dominus servos in agris laborantes spectabat. (6)

7 mater filium in via ludentem vidit. (6)

8 mater filios in via ludentes vidit. (6)

9 rex cives oppidum defendentes laudavit. (5)

10 agricola equum suum ex agro currentem vidit. (7)

Total: 55

Exercise 6.7

Translate the following into English:

1 puer puellam e villa exeuntem vidit. (6)

2 servi dominum iterum clamantem audiverunt. (5)

3 miles in muro stans magna voce clamabat. (7)

4 milites in muro stantes magna voce clamabant. (7)

5 servus in agris laborans multos equos vidit. (7)

6 servi in agris laborantes multos equos viderunt. (7)

7 pater filiam suam vinum bibentem conspexit. (6)

8 dominus ancillam cenam parantem laudavit. (5)

9 dominus ancillas cenam parantes laudavit. (5)

10 dominus crudelis servum effugientem occidit. (5)

Total: 60

→ Revision

Exercise 6.8

Give the translation, person, number, tense, voice and the 1st person singular of the present active of the following verbs:

1 coactus est.

2 ferimur.

3 feremur.

4 posuerunt.

5 rexerunt.

6 potuerunt.

7 amaveramus.

8 videbimur.

9 voluerunt.

10 currebant.

6 marks for each question. Total: 60

Exercise 6.9

Give and translate the following verb parts:

1 The 3rd person singular, perfect active of scribo.

2 The 1st person plural, imperfect passive of cogo.

3 The 3rd person singular, imperfect active of sum.

4 The 1st person singular, perfect passive of punio.

5 The 2nd person plural, perfect active of eo.

6 The 3rd person plural, future passive of video.

7 The 1st person plural, present active of audio.

8 The 2nd person singular, present passive of specto.

9 The 1st person plural, present active of nolo.

10 The 3rd person singular, imperfect passive of porto.

2 marks for each question. Total: 20

Exercise 6.10

Translate the following into Latin:

1 I saw the teacher approaching.

2 I heard the women shouting.

3 We saw the ships approaching.

4 I see the slave working.

5 I saw the slaves hurrying.

3 marks for each question. Total: 15

Exercise 6.11

Translate the following into Latin:

1 The teacher was shouting as he was approaching.   (3)

2 The master saw the slave running out of the villa.   (6)

3 The man saw the girl as he was walking along the road.   (6)

4 We looked at the horses running in the field.   (5)

5 The soldiers were killed as they were escaping from the city.   (5)

Total: 25

Exercise 6.12

Translate the following into English:

1 equi a multis puellis amantur.   (5)

2 nihil melius est quam vinum optimum.   (6)

3 Marcus discipulus peior est quam Sextus.   (6)

4 ad parvam insulam cras omnes navigabimus.   (6)

5 illa puella pulchra a multis pueris amatur.   (7)

Total: 30

Exercise 6.13

Translate the following into Latin:

1 The Greeks were collecting great forces.   (4)

2 The Romans attacked the great city with their weapons.   (5)

3 Many ships were sailing.   (3)

4 Good generals praise brave soldiers.   (5)

5 We looked at the famous temples.   (3)

Total: 20

Exercise 7.1

Translate the following passage. Line numbers are given on the left. New words are underlined in the text and their meanings given in the margin.

Odysseus and his men get a surprise

1 Ulixes comitesque a Lotophagis effugerant. multos dies multasque noctes navigaverunt. tandem, ventis et undis pulsi, ad terram advenerunt. in eadem terra gens gigantum
5 habitabat. Graeci e navibus descenderunt ut cenam in litore pararent. deinde omnem noctem dormiverunt.

prima luce e somno surrexerunt. Ulixes et duodecim amici, ubi gladios et tela collegerunt,
10 e litore discesserunt ut cibum aquamque quaererent. mox ad antrum, in quo multum cibi erat, advenerunt. Graeci, hoc cibo viso, laetissimi erant. cibum ad naves ferre constituerunt ne fame perirent. Ulixes amicis
15 imperavit ut festinarent. Graeci tamen, dum cibum ad naves ferunt, gigantem ingentem appropinquantem viderunt.

Lotophagi, -orum, m. pl. = Lotus
Eaters
nox, noctis, f. = night
pulsi = driven
idem, eadem, idem = the same
gigas, gigantis, m. = giant
ut = to, in order to
litus, litoris, n. = beach
somnus, -i, m. = sleep
surgo, -ere, surrexi, surrectum
(3) = I get up
quaero, -ere, quaesivi,
quaesitum (3) = I look for
antrum, -i, n. = cave
viso = (having been) seen
ne = in order not to
fame = from hunger
impero, -are, imperavi,
imperatum + dative = I order
dum = while

Total: 80

Exercise 7.2

1 From the passage give an example of:

(a) a relative pronoun. (1)

(b) a cardinal number. (1)

(c) a present participle. (1)

2 navibus (line 5). In which case is this noun? Why is this case used? (2)

3 collegerunt (line 9). Give the person, number and tense of this verb.

Give the first person singular of the present tense of this verb. (4)

4 aquam (line 10). Give the gender of this noun. (1)

Total: 10

→ Imperfect subjunctive and purpose clauses

The imperfect subjunctive is regularly used in purpose clauses:

Examples

Main clause	Purpose clause
venimus	ut **laboraremus**.
We came	in order to work.
milites venerunt	ut **pugnarent**.
The soldiers came	to fight.
servus currebat	ne **laboraret**.
The slave was running	in order not to work.

Exercise 7.3

Translate the following into English:

1 servi currebant ut effugerent. (4)

2 servi currebant ne laborarent. (4)

3 viri celeriter effugerunt ne perirent. (5)

4 viri effugerunt ne a gigante interficerentur. (6)

5 pueri ad urbem venerunt ut reginam viderent. (7)

6 cives diu pugnabant ut urbem defenderent. (7)

7 magister multos libros legebat ut sapiens esset. (7)

8 magister clamabat ut a discipulis audiretur. (6)

9 servus currebat ne a domino puniretur. (6)

10 milites Romani fortiter pugnaverunt ut hostes vincerent. (8)

Total: 60

Exercise 7.4

Translate the following into English:

1 Paris ex urbe Troia discessit ut ad Menelaum veniret. (9)

2 Paris Helenam cepit ut eam ad urbem Troiam duceret. (9)

3 Menelaus auxilium amicorum rogavit ut magnas copias colligeret. (8)

4 Menelaus magnas copias collegit ut Troiam oppugnaret. (7)

5 Graeci Troiam oppugnaverunt ut Paridem punirent. (6)

6 Graeci fortiter pugnaverunt ut urbem caperent. (6)

7 Troiani fortiter pugnaverunt ut urbem servarent. (6)

8 Troiani fortiter pugnaverunt ne a Graecis superarentur. (7)

9 tandem Graeci equum ingentem aedificaverunt ut urbem delerent. (8)

10 multi Troiani ex urbe cucurrerunt ut e periculo effugerent. (9)

Total: 75

Exercise 7.5

Translate the following into Latin:

1 The little girls were afraid of the long nights. (5)
2 The women and the old men were escaping. (4)
3 I have seen the famous chieftain. (3)
4 The bright light frightens the girl. (4)
5 The slave is carrying a dead body. (4)

Total: 20

→ Revision

Exercise 7.6

Give the person, number, tense, mood,* voice and the 1st person singular of the present indicative active of the following verbs:

1 possent.
2 collegerunt.
3 duxit.
4 monetur.
5 terrebam.

6 interficeretur.
7 intraverat.
8 dixistis.
9 fert.
10 vulneraret.

* mood: i.e. indicative or subjunctive

6 marks for each question. Total: 60

Exercise 7.7

Give the following verb parts:

1 The 3rd person singular, imperfect subjunctive active of festino.
2 The 1st person singular, imperfect subjunctive passive of video.
3 The 3rd person plural, imperfect subjunctive active of lego.
4 The 2nd person singular, imperfect subjunctive passive of punio.
5 The 1st person plural, imperfect subjunctive active of sum.

1 mark for each question. Total: 5

Exercise 7.8

Give and translate the following:

1 The 3rd person singular, perfect indicative active of iubeo.
2 The 3rd person plural, perfect indicative active of pono.
3 The 1st person plural, perfect indicative active of sto.
4 The 1st person plural, future indicative passive of conspicio.
5 The 3rd person singular, imperfect indicative active of possum.

2 marks for each question. Total: 10

Chapter 7

Exercise 7.9

Give and translate the following:

1   The 3rd person plural, pluperfect indicative active of **sum**.

2   The 1st person plural, perfect indicative active of **eo**.

3   The 2nd person singular, present indicative active of **volo**.

4   The 2nd person singular, imperfect indicative active of **nolo**.

5   The 1st person singular, perfect indicative passive of **porto**.

2 marks for each question. Total: 10

Exercise 7.10

Translate the following into Latin:

1   The pupils were working in order not to be punished by the teacher.

2   The old man was eating food in order to be strong.

3   The boys were reading books in order to be wise.

4   We came to look at the new city.

5   I ran so that the teacher would not see me playing.

6 marks for each question. Total: 30

Exercise 7.11

Translate the following into Latin:

1   We work in the same city.

2   Not everyone likes the same things.

3   They live in the same street.

4   I saw the same boys yesterday.

5   I gave money to the same girl.

4 marks for each question. Total: 20

Exercise 7.12

Translate the following into Latin:

1   We all like the same wine.

2   Teachers always say the same things.

3   The same boys are always fighting.

4   I have already punished the same slave.

5   We are fighting against the same enemy.

4 marks for each question. Total: 20

Exercise 7.13

Translate the following into Latin:

1 I ran in order to arrive soon. (4)

2 He came to the city to see the queen. (6)

3 The slave was running in order to escape from his master. (6)

4 The boy ran in order not to be seen by his father. (6)

5 The young men went to the city to see the beautiful girls. (8)

Total: 30

Exercise 7.14

Put into the plural and translate your answer:

1 noctem semper timeo. (2 + 3)

2 militem audacem amo. (3 + 3)

3 hic miles bellum amabat. (4 + 4)

4 dux a cive laudabatur. (3 + 4)

5 vox a custode audita est. (4 + 5)

Total: 35

Exercise 7.15

Put into the singular and translate your answer:

1 tandem capti sunt. (2 + 3)

2 puellas pulchras spectant. (3 + 3)

3 filiae a matribus saepe monentur. (3 + 5)

4 naves ad insulas pulsae sunt. (4 + 5)

5 senes a servis custodiebantur. (3 + 4)

Total: 35

Exercise 7.16

Translate the following into English:

1 tu plus pecuniae quam ego semper habes. (7)

2 magnam turbam feminarum in urbe vidimus. (6)

3 quod sapiens esse volo, libros semper lego. (7)

4 pecuniam ei heri dedi. (4)

5 multi viri in proeliis saepe occiduntur. (6)

Total: 30

Exercise 8.1

Translate the following passage. Line numbers are given on the left. New words are underlined in the text and their meanings given in the margin.

Trapped by Polyphemus

1 Graeci hunc <u>gigantem</u> <u>visum</u> timebant. <u>sciebant</u>
se in magno periculo iam <u>esse</u>. nomen huius
<u>gigantis</u> Polyphemus erat. altissimus et
<u>ferocissimus</u> et <u>superbissimus</u> erat. unum
5 <u>oculum</u> in medio <u>capite</u> habebat. Ulixes, ubi
Polyphemum appropinquantem vidit, Graecis
<u>facile</u> <u>persuasit</u> <u>ut</u> ad <u>antrum</u> redirent. eis
<u>imperavit</u> <u>ut</u> festinarent, ne a Polyphemo
conspicerentur. Graeci igitur ad <u>antrum</u> celeriter
10 contenderunt. in <u>antro</u> <u>se celabant</u>, nihil
dicentes et Polyphemum <u>exspectantes</u>. <u>ipse</u>
mox advenit. in <u>antrum</u> intravit. deinde <u>exitum</u>
<u>antri</u> <u>saxo</u> ingenti <u>clausit</u>. <u>hoc facto</u>, <u>ignem</u> fecit.
luce <u>flammarum</u> Graecos conspexit. Graeci
15 viderunt Polyphemum iratissimum <u>esse</u>.

gigas, gigantis, m. = giant
visum = (having been) seen
scio, -ire, scivi, scitum (4) = I know
esse = were
ferox, ferocis = fierce
superbus, -a, -um = proud, arrogant
oculus, -i, m. = eye
caput, capitis, n. = head
facile = easily
persuadeo, -ere, persuasi, persuasum + dative (2) = I persuade
ut = to
antrum, -i, n. = cave
impero, -are, imperavi + dative (1) = I order
me celo, -are, -avi, -atum (1) = I hide (myself)
exspecto, -are, -avi, -atum (1) = I wait for
ipse = he/himself
exitus, -us, m. = exit
saxum, -i, n. = rock
claudo, -ere, clausi, clausum (3) = I shut
hoc facto = with this done
ignis, ignis, m. = fire
flamma, -ae, f. = flame
esse = was

Total: 60

Exercise 8.2

1 From the passage give an example of:

   (a) a reflexive pronoun. (1)

   (b) an adverb. (1)

   (c) a superlative adjective. (1)

2 esse (line 2). What part of the verb sum is this? (1)

3 oculum (line 5). In which case is this noun? Why is this case used? (2)

4   fecit (line 13). Give the person, number and tense of this verb.

Give the 1st person singular of the present tense of this verb.   (4)

Total: 10

→ Indirect commands

Latin: Main clause as usual + **ut** (to); **ne** (not to).

In the past, the verb of the indirect command is in the imperfect subjunctive, rather like a purpose clause.

> **Reminder:** a very common verb used in this construction is **impero** (1) + dat., I order. The person or persons being ordered must be in the dative case in Latin.

Examples

Main clause	Indirect command
dux militibus imperavit The general ordered the soldiers	ut oppugnarent. to attack.
dux militibus imperavit The general ordered the soldiers	ne oppugnarent. not to attack.

But note that the verb **iubeo** is followed by a simple infinitive:

Example

dux milites oppugnare iussit.

The general ordered the soldiers to attack.

Translate the following indirect commands (the main clause is the same in each case):

Exercise 8.3

	Main clause	Indirect command	
1	dux militibus imperavit	ut bene pugnarent.	(4)
2		ut oppidum oppugnarent.	(3)
3		ut urbem fortiter defenderent.	(4)
4		ne hostes timerent.	(3)
5		ne ab hostibus vincerentur.	(4)
6		ut reginam audirent.	(3)
7		ne dormirent.	(2)
8		ut oppidum delerent.	(3)
9		ne currerent.	(2)
10		ne caperentur.	(2)

Total: 30

Exercise 8.4

	Main clause	Indirect command	
1	dominus servo persuasit	ut laboraret.	(5)
2		ne luderet.	(2)
3		ut cibum pararet.	(3)
4		ut ad urbem iret.	(4)
5		ut librum legeret.	(3)
6		ne dormiret.	(2)
7		ne timeret.	(2)
8		ut aquam biberet.	(3)
9		ne vinum biberet.	(3)
10		ut bonus esset.	(3)

Total: 30

Exercise 8.5

Translate the following into English:

1 dux nautis imperavit ut naves aedificarent. (6)

2 dux militibus imperavit ut fortiter pugnarent. (6)

3 dominus servum monuit ne hoc faceret. (6)

4 magister discipulos saepe monebat ut laborarent. (6)

5 pater me monuit ne illum librum legerem. (7)

6 dominus mihi persuasit ut manerem. (5)

7 dominus servo imperavit ut cenam pararet. (6)

8 te monui ne superbus esses. (5)

9 mater filium rogavit ne ad urbem iret. (7)

10 dux militibus imperavit ut oppidum oppugnarent. (6)

Total: 60

Exercise 8.6

Translate the following into English:

1 regina civibus persuasit ut bene laborarent. (6)

2 pater filiam monuit ne in media via luderet. (8)

3 magistrum rogavimus ut statim discederet. (5)

4 dux militibus persuasit ne hostes timerent. (6)

5 vir uxori persuasit ut ad urbem secum iret. (8)

Chapter 8

6 eum monui ut hoc statim faceret. (6)

7 mater filiam monuit ne per vias urbis nocte ambularet. (9)

8 puero imperavi ut laboraret. (4)

9 patri persuasi ut pecuniam mihi daret. (6)

10 uxor domino persuasit ut illum servum liberaret. (7)

Total: 65

→ Revision

Exercise 8.7

Translate the following into Latin:

1 Proud soldiers do not fear wars. (5)

2 Pupils do not like cruel teachers. (5)

3 Many ships were approaching. (3)

4 The daring soldier fought with great bravery. (5)

5 The slave was escaping. (2)

Total: 20

Exercise 8.8

Give the person, number, tense, mood, voice and the 1st person singular of the present indicative active of the following verbs:

1 videretur.

2 iremus.

3 imperabo.

4 vocabimur.

5 occidit.

6 esset.

7 persuasimus.

8 defenderent.

9 missus est.

10 vocabamur.

6 marks for each question. Total: 60

Exercise 8.9

Give the following verb parts:

1 The 3rd person plural, imperfect subjunctive active of **facio**.

2 The 3rd person singular, imperfect subjunctive passive of **occido**.

3 The 1st person plural, imperfect subjunctive active of **possum**.

4 The 2nd person singular, imperfect subjunctive passive of **porto**.

5 The 3rd person plural, imperfect subjunctive active of **eo**.

1 mark for each question. Total: 5

Exercise 8.10

Give and translate the following:

1 The 1st person singular, future indicative active of **constituo**.

2 The 1st person plural, imperfect indicative active of **festino**.

3 The 3rd person singular, future indicative passive of **do**.

4 The 3rd person singular, perfect indicative active of **fero**.

5 The 2nd person plural, imperfect indicative passive of **cogo**.

6 The 2nd person singular, future indicative active of **persuadeo**.

7 The 1st person singular, perfect indicative active of **impero**.

8 The 3rd person plural, perfect indicative active of **fugio**.

9 The 3rd person singular, perfect indicative passive of **deleo**.

10 The 3rd person plural, pluperfect indicative passive of **oppugno**.

2 marks for each question. Total: 20

Exercise 8.11

Translate the following into Latin:

1 I asked every pupil to work.

2 I asked the wise pupils to work.

3 I persuaded the boy not to do this.

4 I persuaded the boys not to do this.

5 He ordered the slave to hurry.

4 marks for each question. Total: 20

Exercise 8.12

Translate the following into Latin:

1 The master ordered the slaves to hurry. (5)

2 The general ordered the soldier to be brave. (5)

3 The general ordered the soldiers to fight. (4)

4 The teacher ordered the pupil to work. (5)

5 The girl asked her mother to give money to the slave. (6)

Total: 25

Exercise 8.13

Translate the following into English:

1 puella quam heri spectabam pulcherrima erat. (6)

2 omnes milites verbis ducis territi erant. (6)

3 curremus. (1)

4 filius auxilium rogare coactus est. (5)

5 omnia scio. (2)

Total: 20

Exercise 9.1

Translate the following passage. Line numbers are given on the left. New words are underlined in the text and their meanings given in the margin.

Panic!

1 Graeci, in <u>antro clausi</u>, timebant. Ulixes <u>sciebat</u>
se comitesque suos in magno periculo <u>esse</u>.
Polyphemus, Graecis <u>conspectis</u>, iratissimus
erat. magna voce clamavit: 'hoc <u>antrum</u> meum,
5 non vestrum, est. cur hic adestis?'

his verbis <u>auditis</u>, Graeci omnem <u>spem</u>
<u>deposuerunt</u>. Ulixes autem comites monuit ne
timerent et haec verba Polyphemo <u>locutus est</u>:
'milites Graeci sumus. a nobis urbs Troia capta
10 est. ad Graeciam redimus ut <u>familias</u> nostras
iterum videamus. nos <u>iuva</u>! cibum aquamque
<u>petimus</u>. da cibum nobis, deinde <u>proficiscemur</u>.'

ille, hoc audito, nihil dixit. <u>animal</u> crudele erat.
duos e Graecis in <u>manu</u> cepit, capita eorum
15 contra <u>saxum fregit</u>, statim eos consumpsit.
ceteri Graeci nihil facere poterant.

antrum, -i, n. = cave
claudo, -ere, clausi, clausum
(3) = I shut
scio, scire, scivi, scitum (4)
= I know
esse = were
conspectis = (having been)
caught sight of
auditis = (having been) heard
spes, spei, f. = hope
depono, -ere, deposui,
depositum (3) = I give up
locutus est = spoke
familia, -ae, f. = family
iuvo, -are, iuvi, iutum (1) =
I help
peto, -ere, petivi, petitum (3)
= I seek
proficiscemur = we shall set
off
animal, animalis, n. = animal
manu = hand
saxum, -i, n. = rock
frango, -ere, fregi, fractum
(3) = I smash

Total: 75

Exercise 9.2

1 From the passage give an example of:

(a) a reflexive pronoun. (1)

(b) an imperative. (1)

(c) a verb in the subjunctive. (1)

(d) an infinitive. (1)

2 nobis (line 9). In which case is this pronoun? Why is this case used? (2)

3 cepit (line 14). Give the person, number and tense of this verb.

Give the first person singular of the present tense of this verb. (4)

Total: 10

→ Past participle passive

The PPP in English: a reminder

Translating the PPP as **having been -d** can sometimes lead to unnatural English. The English can be improved by getting rid of the **having been** and replacing it with **when**, **since** or a main verb + and ...

> **Example**
>
> urbs **capta** deleta est.
>
> (Literally: The **having-been-captured** city was destroyed.)
>
> These sound more natural:
>
> > **When** the city was captured it was destroyed.
> >
> > The city **was** captured and destroyed.

At the beginning of the passage above we read:

Graeci, in antro **clausi**, timebant.
The Greeks, **having-been-shut** in the cave, were afraid.

How might you improve the English here, by getting rid of the **having been**?

Exercise 9.3

Translate the following into English:

1 oppidum captum deletum est.	(4)
2 servi capti a domino puniti sunt.	(6)
3 discipuli, a magistro moniti, riserunt.	(5)
4 servus, a domino liberatus, laetissimus erat.	(6)
5 Graeci victi a Romanis capti sunt.	(6)
6 puella, ab amicis relicta, flebat.	(5)
7 milites, a duce laudati, praemia acceperunt.	(6)
8 cena, ab ancilla parata, ab omnibus laudata est.	(8)
9 terra, a Romanis capta, bene regebatur.	(6)
10 servi, a domino laborare iussi, non laeti erant.	(8)

Total: 60

Exercise 9.4

Translate the following into English:

1 Helena, a Paride visa, ad urbem Troiam ducta est.	(9)
2 multae naves paratae ad Menelaum missae sunt.	(7)
3 Troia, a Graecis oppugnata, a civibus diu defendebatur.	(8)
4 urbs diu oppugnata tandem capta est.	(6)
5 multi cives, ab hostibus vulnerati, ex urbe fugerunt.	(8)

6 equus ingens, a Graecis aedificatus, prope urbem relictus est. (9)

7 equus, prope urbem relictus, a Troianis visus est. (8)

8 equus, a Troianis visus, in urbem ductus est. (8)

9 Troia, a Graecis capta, tandem deleta est. (7)

10 naves, tempestate deletae, numquam redierunt. (5)

Total: 75

Exercise 9.5

Translate the following into English:

1 puer puellam visam amavit. (4)

2 puella puerum visum amavit. (4)

3 vir librum acceptum legit. (4)

4 hostes urbem oppugnatam ceperunt. (4)

5 hostes urbem captam deleverunt. (4)

6 Romani Graecos vulneratos occiderunt. (4)

7 servus cibum captum consumpsit. (4)

8 Menelaus copias paratas ad urbem Troiam misit. (7)

9 Graeci Polyphemum visum timebant. (4)

10 pater filium punitum e villa misit. (6)

Total: 45

Exercise 9.6

Translate the following into English:

1 socii naves paratas ad Menelaum statim miserunt. (7)

2 poeta librum longum scriptum ad omnes amicos misit. (8)

3 Graeci equum ingentem aedificatum prope urbem reliquerunt. (7)

4 Troiani equum visum in urbem duxerunt. (6)

5 discipuli verba a magistro dicta non audiverunt. (7)

6 milites tela celeriter parata in hostes miserunt. (7)

7 Romani servos a Graecis captos liberaverunt. (6)

8 subito Polyphemus duos Graecos captos consumpsit. (6)

9 hunc librum mihi datum iam legi. (6)

10 cenam ab ancilla paratam laudavimus. (5)

Total: 65

Exercise 9.7

Translate the following into Latin:

1 We heard loud shouts. (3)

2 The angry general punished all the bad soldiers. (6)

3 The enemy killed the guards with their weapons. (4)

4 Farmers like a beautiful day. (4)

5 My mother is crying. (3)

Total: 20

Exercise 9.8

Give the person, number, tense, mood, voice and the 1st person singular of the present indicative active of the following verbs:

1 veniam.

2 iuvat.

3 scripserunt.

4 servaretur.

5 tenebatur.

6 vinceremur.

7 pugnabamus.

8 redibimus.

9 staret.

10 traditus est.

6 marks for each question. Total: 60

Exercise 9.9

Give the following verb parts:

1 The 3rd person singular, imperfect subjunctive active of volo.

2 The 2nd person singular, imperfect subjunctive passive of rego.

3 The 3rd person plural, imperfect subjunctive active of nolo.

4 The 3rd person plural, imperfect subjunctive passive of conspicio.

5 The 1st person plural, imperfect subjunctive active of sum.

1 mark for each question. Total: 5

Exercise 9.10

Give and translate the following verb parts:

1 The 3rd person plural, future indicative active of venio.

2 The 2nd person singular, perfect indicative active of rideo.

3 The 1st person plural, future indicative passive of iuvo.

4 The 3rd person plural, pluperfect indicative active of pugno.

5 The 3rd person singular, perfect indicative active of video.

6 The 3rd person plural, imperfect indicative active of **sedeo**.

7 The 1st person singular, perfect indicative passive of **vinco**.

8 The 1st person singular, perfect indicative active of **scribo**.

9 The 3rd person plural, perfect indicative active of **trado**.

10 The 1st person plural, imperfect indicative active of **sum**.

2 marks for each question. Total: 20

Exercise 9.11

Translate the following into Latin:

1 The girl, punished by the angry teacher, was crying. (6)

2 The boys, seen by their father, ran into the fields. (7)

3 The soldier, captured by the enemy, was killed. (5)

4 The ships, prepared by the Romans, departed immediately. (6)

5 The weapons, collected by the slaves, were new. (6)

Total: 30

Exercise 9.12

Translate the following into Latin:

1 The cruel master punished the slave and killed him.

2 The pupils saw the master and did not like him.

3 The soldiers saw the guards and killed them with their swords.

4 We heard the girl's voice and liked it immediately.

5 The man read the book and gave it to me.

5 marks for each question. Total: 25

Exercise 9.13

Translate the following into English:

1 multae gentes Romanos non amabant. (5)

2 hic agricola plures equos quam ille habet. (7)

3 illa urbs ab hostibus diu oppugnabatur. (6)

4 urbs Troia tandem decimo anno capta est. (7)

5 nautae ab insula hodie navigabunt. (5)

Total: 30

Exercise 10.1

Translate the following passage. Line numbers are given on the left. New words are underlined in the text and their meanings given in the margin.

Polyphemus is tricked by Odysseus

1 omnes Graeci magnopere timebant. iam
viderant Polyphemum animal crudelissimum
esse. Ulixes, qui audacissimus Graecorum erat,
Polyphemum dolo superare constituit. poculum
5 vino plenum ferens, ad gigantem appropinquavit.

'bibe hoc vinum, Polypheme. dulcissimum est.'

gigas vinum captum statim bibit. deinde Ulixi
clamavit: 'hoc vinum optimum est. da mihi plus vini!'

Ulixes ei poculum secundum, deinde tertium,
10 deinde quartum dedit. Polyphemus iam ebrius
erat. ad terram subito cecidit et obdormivit.
Graeci, ubi viderunt Polyphemum dormire,
palum ceperunt et in oculum gigantis truserunt.
ille statim surrexit, magna voce clamans.
15 caecus et iratissimus erat. Graeci ex antro
effugere cupiebant.

esse = was
dolus, -i, m. = trickery

poculum, -i, n. = goblet
plenus, -a, -um, + ablative
= full of

gigas, gigantis, m. = giant
dulcis, -is, -e = sweet

ebrius, -a, -um = drunk
cado, -ere, cecidi, casum
(3) = I fall
obdormio, -ire,
obdormivi, -itum (4) =
I fall asleep
dormire = was sleeping
palus, -i, m. = a stake
oculus, -i, m. = eye
trudo, -ere, trusi, trusum
(3) = I thrust
surgo, -ere, surrexi,
surrectum (3) = I get up
caecus, -a, -um = blind
antrum, - i, n. = cave

Total: 75

Exercise 10.2

1 From the passage give an example of:

(a) a relative pronoun. (1)

(b) a present participle. (1)

(c) an ordinal number. (1)

2 optimum (line 8). This is a superlative adjective. Give its positive
form in the nominative masculine singular. (1)

3 dedit (line 10). Give the person, number and tense of this verb.
Give the 1st person singular of the present indicative active of this verb. (4)

4 terram (line 11). In which case is this noun? Why is this case used? (2)

Total: 10

→ Place

Motion towards is expressed by the accusative and motion from is expressed by the ablative. Position 'where' is expressed by a preposition. But note that the rules vary a bit when cities and small islands are involved.

	at	towards	from
most nouns	prepositions + ablative	prepositions + accusative	prepositions + ablative
	in agro	ad agrum	ex agro
	in the field	to the field	out of the field
cities and small islands	locative – special ending	accusative only	ablative only
	Romae	Romam	Roma
	in Rome, at Rome	to Rome	from Rome
two special nouns:			
domus (home)	domi	domum	domo
	at home	(to) home	from home
rus (country)*	ruri	rus	rure
	in the country	to the country	from the country

* not required for Common Entrance

Exercise 10.3

Translate the following into English:

1 omnes agricolae ruri habitant. (4)

2 dux Roma prima luce discessit. (5)

3 equi ex agris currebant. (4)

4 rus cras ibimus. (3)

5 puer domo discessit et ad urbem festinavit. (7)

6 multi cives Romae habitabant. (4)

7 servi rure Romam festinabant. (4)

8 pater et filius domum ibant. (5)

9 milites Roma cras discedent. (4)

10 puer et puella domi manebant. (5)

Total: 45

Exercise 10.4

Translate the following into Latin:

1 The guards ran quickly.

2 The storm was very big.

3 Many animals were running.

4 The ships were quick.

5 The house is small.

3 marks for each question. Total: 15

Exercise 10.5

Translate the following into Latin:

1 The chieftains will meet tomorrow. (3)

2 The slaves were guarding the house. (3)

3 I like sleep. (2)

4 Slaves often seek rewards. (4)

5 A storm destroyed the ship. (3)

Total: 15

Exercise 10.6

Translate the following into English:

1 servi effugere coacti sunt. (4)

2 animalia cibum frustra petebant. (4)

3 multae naves illa tempestate deletae sunt. (6)

4 dominus illum servum punire nolebat. (5)

5 senex per vias multos dies ambulabat. (6)

Total: 25

Exercise 10.7

Translate the following into English:

1 aqua in villam a servo ferebatur. (6)

2 domini servis non saepe credunt. (5)

3 urbs ab hostibus multos annos oppugnabatur. (6)

4 senes laborare saepe nolunt. (4)

5 non omnes bene cantamus. (4)

Total: 25

Exercise 10.8

Translate the following into English:

1 milites multa animalia sagittis interfecerunt. (5)

2 multa animalia a militibus sagittis interfecta sunt. (7)

3 nonne Graeci urbem Troiam multos annos oppugnabant? (7)

4 noli hoc iterum facere, iuvenis! (5)

5 Graeci milites meliores quam Troiani erant. (6)

Total: 30

Exercise 10.9

Give the translation, person, number, tense, voice and the 1st person singular of the present indicative active of the following verbs:

1 iuvabit.

2 persuaserunt.

3 imperavit.

4 coacti sumus.

5 latus erat.

6 custodiebatur.

7 volet.

8 pepulimus.

9 petiverunt.

10 interficiam.

6 marks for each question. Total: 60

Exercise 10.10

Give and translate the following verb parts:

1 The 1st person plural, present indicative active of nolo.

2 The 3rd person singular, perfect indicative active of cogo.

3 The 3rd person plural, perfect indicative passive of fero.

4 The 2nd person singular, perfect indicative active of custodio.

5 The 3rd person plural, imperfect indicative active of volo.

1 mark for each question. Total: 5

Exercise 10.11

Give and translate the following verb parts:

1 The 1st person singular, future indicative active of peto.

2 The 3rd person singular, perfect indicative passive of pello.

3 The 3rd person singular, perfect indicative active of credo.

4 The 3rd person plural, perfect indicative active of convenio.

5 The 2nd person singular, imperfect indicative active of possum.

1 mark for each question. Total: 5

Exercise 10.12

Translate the following into English:

1 magister pueris imperavit ut laborarent. (5)

2 Troiani multos Graecos appropinquantes viderunt. (5)

3 hostes media nocte appropinquabant ut urbem oppugnarent. (7)

4 filius, a patre monitus, hoc iterum non fecit. (8)

5 omnes omnia facere non possumus. (5)

Total: 30

Exercise 10.13

Translate the following into English:

1 quis puerum qui hoc fecit vidit? (6)

2 urbs a civibus bene defendebatur. (5)

3 ancillae a domino cenam parare coactae erant. (7)

4 illi milites quos vides fortissimi sunt. (6)

5 dux militibus persuasit ut hoc facerent. (6)

Total: 30

Exercise 10.14

Put into the plural and translate your answer:

1 senex lente currebat. (2 + 3)

2 tandem miles interfectus est. (3 + 4)

3 puella a servo fortiter custodiebatur. (3 + 5)

4 iuvenis pugnare nolebat. (2 + 3)

5 hoc vinum est quod amo. (5 + 5)

Total: 35

Exercise 10.15

Put into the singular and translate your answer:

1 animalia effugiebant. (2 + 2)

2 templa deleta erant. (3 + 3)

3 illi domini hos servos puniunt. (5 + 5)

4 scuta a iuvenibus et servis portabantur. (4 + 6)

5 viri saepe sapientiores quam mulieres sunt. (4 + 6)

Total: 40

Exercise 10.16

Translate the following into Latin:

1 In that war many men were killed. (6)
2 The beautiful girl was being watched by many boys. (6)
3 Many wounds were received by the soldiers in that battle. (8)
4 Ships are not often destroyed by storms. (5)
5 The city had been attacked by the Greeks for a long time. (5)

Total: 30

Exercise 10.17

Translate the following into Latin:

1 My friend's sister likes horses. (5)
2 The bold young men killed the king in the city. (6)
3 Slaves were carrying the bodies out of the town. (5)
4 The master will hand over the money to his best slaves. (5)
5 The enemy's forces had beaten the Romans. (4)

Total: 25

Exercise 10.18

Translate the following into Latin:

1 Because of the delay, many slaves were wounded.
2 The soldiers were often praised by the general.
3 Food will be given to the slave by the master tomorrow.
4 Teachers are not often liked by their pupils.
5 Many weapons had been found near the city.

6 marks for each question. Total: 30

Exercise 10.19

Translate the following into Latin:

1 Many old men were shouting in the streets. (5)
2 The queen praised the soldier's courage. (4)
3 The slaves will guard the king well. (4)
4 Boys do not often find money in the street. (7)
5 The old man had loved many beautiful women. (5)

Total: 25

Chapter 10

Exercise 10.20

Translate the following into English:

1 ad urbem celeriter currere debes.   (6)

2 multis sagittis vulnerata erat.   (4)

3 multi amici vobiscum mox venient.   (5)

4 te hoc statim facere iubeo.   (5)

5 cena optima a femina parabatur.   (5)

Total: 25

(End of Common Entrance Level 3 prescription)

Exercise 11.1

Translate the following passage. Line numbers are given on the left. New words are underlined in the text and their meanings given in the margin.

The Greeks escape from Polyphemus and reach the island of Aeolia

1 Graeci, Polyphemo vulnerato, timebant.
Polyphemus ipse iratissimus erat. sciebat
Graecos ex antro effugere velle. saxo ab exitu
antri remoto, ipse in exitu stetit, ut Graecos,
5 effugere conantes, caperet. non tamen potuit.
Graeci, sub ventribus ovium suspensi, ex antro
exierunt. hoc facto, ad navem celeriter
cucurrerunt. sciebant se tutos iam esse.

Graeci multos dies navigaverunt. ad insulam
10 Aeoliam tandem advenerunt. hic habitabat
Aeolus, rex ventorum. Ulixes eum rogavit ut
auxilium sibi et comitibus daret. Aeolus,
omnibus ventis in sacco positis, haec verba
Ulixi dixit: 'cape hunc saccum. auxilio horum
15 ventorum ad Graeciam redire poteritis.' his
verbis dictis Aeolus saccum ventorum Ulixi
tradidit. Ulixes, sacco accepto, ex insula Aeolia
statim discessit.

scio, -ire, scivi, scitum (4) = I know
antrum, -i, n. = cave
saxum, -i, n. = rock
exitus, -us, m. = exit
removeo, -ere, removi, removtum (2) = I remove
conantes = trying
venter, ventris, m. = belly
ovis, -is, f. = sheep
suspensi = hanging
esse = were

saccus, -i, m. = bag

Total: 90

Exercise 11.2

1 From the passage give an example of:

(a) a superlative adjective. (1)

(b) an infinitive. (1)

(c) an imperative. (1)

(d) a preposition. (1)

2 ventorum (line 15). Give the gender and case of this noun. (2)

3 poteritis (line 15). Give the person, number, tense and the 1st person singular of the present tense of this verb. (4)

Total: 10

→ Ablative absolute

This usually consists of a past participle passive (PPP) agreeing with a noun in the ablative. Its literal meaning of **with something having-been-done** can usually be turned into better English by using **when ... had been ...** or a main verb + and.

> **Examples**
> 1 domino viso, servi fugerunt.
>   (Poor English: With the master having-been-seen, the slaves fled.)
>   When the master had been seen, the slaves fled.
>   The slaves saw the master and fled.
> 2 host**ibus** vi**sis**, milites timebant.
>   (Poor English: With the enemy having-been-seen, the soldiers were afraid.)
>   When the enemy had been seen, the soldiers were afraid.
>   The soldiers saw the enemy and were afraid.

Exercise 11.3

Translate the following ablative absolute constructions using the 'when ... had been ...' formula mentioned above:

1 clamore audito ...

2 puellis territis ...

3 oppido capto ...

4 urbe deleta ...

5 hostibus victis ...

6 muro aedificato ...

7 matre mea vocata ...

8 turba discedere iussa ...

9 dono accepto ...

10 pecunia tradita ...

11 armis paratis ...

12 libro longo scripto ...

13 his verbis auditis ...

14 incolis miseris servatis ...

15 urbe bene defensa ...

16 armis collectis ...

17 puella in via visa ...

18 discipulis punitis ...

19 multis militibus vulneratis ...

20 muro oppugnato ...

2 marks for each question. Total: 40

Exercise 11.4

Translate the following into English:

1 magister, discipulo punito, risit. (4)

2 multis servis liberatis, dominus laetus erat. (6)

3 puella pulcherrima conspecta, puer laetissimus erat. (6)

4 his verbis dictis, regina discessit. (5)

5 hoc audito, puella magnopere timebat. (5)

6 servi, domino saevo viso, timebant. (5)

7 cibo consumpto, nautae dormiverunt. (4)

8 armis paratis, milites clamantes ruerunt. (5)

9 hoc libro lecto, puella tristis erat. (6)

10 hostibus victis, Romani discesserunt. (4)

Total: 50

Exercise 11.5

Translate the following into English:

1 Helena capta, rex Menelaus iratissimus erat. (6)

2 nuntiis ad multas urbes missis, Menelaus magnas copias collegit. (9)

3 magnis copiis collectis, Menelaus laetus erat. (6)

4 omnibus navibus paratis, Graeci Troiam navigaverunt. (6)

5 Troia decem annos oppugnata, Graeci fessi erant. (7)

6 urbe diu bene defensa, cives Troiani laeti erant. (8)

7 magno equo aedificato, Graeci in navibus discesserunt. (7)

8 magno equo in urbem ducto, cives laetissimi erant. (8)

9 multis civibus occisis, Graeci urbem celeriter ceperunt. (7)

10 urbe capta, Graeci ad Graeciam redierunt. (6)

Total: 70

Exercise 11.6

Translate the following into Latin:

1 The enemy seized the city. (3)

2 The citizens were defending the city with great bravery. (5)

3 The boy's father is very afraid. (4)

4 The slave was escaping from the town. (4)

5 The soldiers fought in the long battle. (4)

Total: 20

Exercise 11.7

Translate the following into Latin:

1 The teacher is liked by the pupils.   (4)

2 The slaves have been punished by the master.   (4)

3 The beautiful girls were being watched by the boys.   (5)

4 Many soldiers were killed in the battle.   (5)

5 The temples are being destroyed.   (2)

Total: 20

Exercise 11.8

Translate the following into Latin:

1 When the soldier had been punished ...

2 When the enemy had been seen ...

3 When the ships had been built ...

4 When the old men had been heard ...

5 When the Romans had been beaten ...

6 When the book had been read ...

7 When the guards had been killed ...

8 When the city had been captured ...

9 When the brave men had been praised ...

10 When the gold had been found ...

2 marks for each question. Total: 20

→ Revision

Exercise 11.9

Give the person, number, tense, mood, voice and the 1st person singular of the present indicative active of the following verbs:

1 oppugnatur.   6 nuntiaret.

2 flevit.   7 fecerat.

3 iacti sunt.   8 effugiam.

4 dederunt.   9 intravit.

5 laudabatur.   10 darent.

6 marks for each question. Total: 60

Exercise 11.10

Give the following verb parts:

1 The 3rd person plural, imperfect subjunctive active of **credo**.

2 The 3rd person singular, imperfect subjunctive passive of **defendo**.

3 The 2nd person plural, imperfect subjunctive active of **video**.

4 The 1st person singular, imperfect subjunctive passive of **vulnero**.

5 The 1st person plural, imperfect subjunctive active of **relinquo**.

1 mark for each question. Total: 5

Exercise 11.11

Give and translate the following verb parts:

1 The 3rd person plural, imperfect indicative passive of **colligo**.

2 The 3rd person singular, imperfect indicative active of **cupio**.

3 The 1st person plural, perfect indicative active of **habeo**.

4 The 3rd person plural, pluperfect indicative active of **curro**.

5 The 3rd person singular, imperfect indicative active of **possum**.

6 The 1st person plural, perfect indicative active of **do**.

7 The 1st person singular, future indicative active of **eo**.

8 The 3rd person plural, perfect indicative active of **discedo**.

9 The 3rd person singular, perfect indicative active of **nolo**.

10 The 3rd person singular, future indicative passive of **capio**.

2 marks for each question. Total: 20

Exercise 11.12

Translate the following into English:

1 Romani in multis proeliis contra hostes pugnaverunt. (7)

2 Romulus oppidum in septem montibus aedificavit. (6)

3 nomen huius oppidi Roma erat. (5)

4 Romani milites meliores quam Graeci erant. (6)

5 multi equi telis hostium vulnerati sunt. (6)

Total: 30

Exercise 12.1

Translate the following passage. Line numbers are given on the left. New words are underlined in the text and their meanings given in the margin.

The Greeks, almost at Ithaca, are driven back to Aeolus

1 Ulixes, sacco ventorum ab Aeolo accepto, ex
insula Aeolia discesserat. cum comitibus ad
insulam Ithacam iam tandem appropinquabat.
comites tamen Ulixis laeti non erant. nesciebant
5 ventos in sacco Ulixi dato inesse; credebant
Ulixem aurum pecuniamque in sacco habere;
dicebant Ulixem virum crudelem avarumque
esse. putabant Ulixem aurum pecuniamque
tenere velle.

10 cum igitur Ulixes fessus dormiret, comites
saccum aperire constituerunt. sacco aperto,
omnes venti e sacco statim effugerunt et navem
ab insula Ithaca pepulerunt. Ulixes, e somno
excitatus, hoc viso, iratissimus erat. clamavit:
15 'cur hoc fecistis? domum paene adveneramus.'
navis ad Aeoliam repulsa est. rex Aeolus
autem auxilium Graecis iterum dare noluit. illi
nihil facere poterant. sciebant Ulixem
iratissimum esse et se stultos fuisse.

Margin glosses:

saccus, -i, m. = bag

nescio, -ire, -ivi, -itum (4)
= I do not know
inesse = were in

avarus, -a, -um = mean
puto, -are, -avi, -atum (1)
= I think

cum = while
aperio, -ire, aperui, apertum
(4) = I open

excito, -are, -avi, -atum
(1) = I wake up
repello, -ere, reppuli,
repulsum (3) = I drive back
scio, -ire, scivi, scitum (4)
= I know
stultus, -a, -um = stupid
fuisse = had been

Total: 100

Exercise 12.2

1 From the passage give an example of:

 (a) an ablative absolute construction. (1)

 (b) a present infinitive. (1)

 (c) a verb in the pluperfect tense. (1)

 (d) a noun in the dative case. (1)

2 comitibus (line 2). In which case is this noun? Why is this case used? (2)

3 velle (line 9). What part of the verb is this? Give the 1st person
singular of the present indicative active of this verb. (2)

4 iratissimum (line 19). This is a superlative adjective. Give the
nominative masculine singular of the positive and comparative forms
of this adjective. (2)

Total: 10

→ Indirect statements: accusative and present infinitive

An indirect statement consists of a **verb** of seeing, hearing, knowing, saying, etc. followed by the word **that**.

> **Examples**
>
> I know **that** you are stupid.
> He heard **that** the teacher was a good one.
> She said **that** she was ill.

In Latin, the subject of the indirect statement goes into the **accusative** case and the verb of the indirect statement goes into the **infinitive**.

> **Examples**
>
> I know that the girl is coming.
> scio puell**am** ven**ire**.
>
> (accusative) (infinitive)
>
> I knew that the girl was coming.
> sciebam puell**am** ven**ire**.
>
> (accusative) (infinitive)

Exercise 12.3

Translate the following into English:

1 video puerum currere.

2 video pueros currere.

3 vidi puerum currere.

4 vidi pueros currere.

5 audio puellam clamare.

6 audio puellas clamare.

7 audivi puellam clamare.

8 audivi puellas clamare.

9 scio milites venire.

10 sciebam milites venire.

3 marks for each question. Total: 30

Exercise 12.4

Translate the following into English:

1 scio hunc servum effugere. (4)

2 scio hos servos effugere. (4)

3 sciebam hunc servum effugere. (4)

4 sciebam hos servos effugere. (4)

5 video omnes discipulos laborare. (4)

6 vidi omnes discipulos laborare. (4)

7 magister scit puerum non laborare. (5)

8 magister sciebat puerum non laborare. (5)

9 pater scit filium pecuniam amare. (5)

10 discipuli sciebant hunc magistrum bonum esse. (6)

Total: 45

Exercise 12.5

Translate the following into English:

1 scio agricolam laborare. (3)

2 scio agricolas laborare. (3)

3 sciebam agricolam laborare. (3)

4 sciebam agricolas laborare. (3)

5 puer dicit puellam pulchram esse. (5)

6 puer dicit puellas pulchras esse. (5)

7 puer dixit puellam pulchram esse. (5)

8 puer dixit puellas pulchras esse. (5)

9 audio magistrum bonum esse. (4)

10 audivi magistrum bonum esse. (4)

Total: 40

Exercise 12.6

Translate the following into English:

1 scimus omnes magistros sapientes esse. (5)

2 video te tandem bene laborare. (5)

3 audio puellam venire. (3)

4 dicunt Romanos oppidum oppugnare. (4)

5 servi sciunt dominum iam appropinquare. (5)

6 dux scit milites fortes esse. (5)

7 magistri sciunt omnes puellas bene laborare. (6)

8 scimus illum virum vocem magnam habere. (6)

9 audio multos servos effugere. (4)

10 Marcus scit Flaviam cenas bonas semper parare. (7)

Total: 50

→ Present infinitive passive

Examples

1 multi magistri a discipulis amari volunt.
   Many teachers want to be liked by their pupils.
2 puer puniri non vult.
   The boy does not want to be punished.

Exercise 12.7

Translate the following into English:

1 dux multa tela iaci iussit.   (5)

2 cives urbem bene defendi volebant.   (5)

3 ab hostibus capi nolumus.   (4)

4 dux cives a servis custodiri iussit.   (6)

5 dominus hunc servum interfici iussit.   (5)

6 Romani ab hostibus vinci numquam volebant.   (6)

7 princeps arma a civibus colligi iussit.   (6)

8 rex pecuniam hostibus tradi iussit.   (5)

9 Graeci urbem novam in hoc loco aedificari iusserunt.   (8)

10 discipuli a magistro puniri nolunt.   (5)

Total: 55

Exercise 12.8

Translate the following into English:

1 Troiani viderunt urbem suam a Graecis oppugnari.   (7)

2 Troiani viderunt se a Graecis vinci.   (6)

3 cives Troiani sciebant urbem capi.   (5)

4 rex vidit templa Troiae a Graecis deleri.   (6)

5 rex vidit multos cives a Graecis occidi.   (7)

6 cives nesciebant equum ingentem a Graecis aedificari.   (7)

7 Graeci viderunt equum in urbem a Troianis duci.   (8)

8 Ulixes audivit comites suos a Lotophagis teneri.   (7)

9 Ulixes sciebat se a deis puniri.   (6)

10 Ulixes vidit naves suas tempestate deleri.   (6)

Total: 65

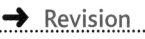

Exercise 12.9

Translate the following into Latin:

1 The soldiers received many wounds. (4)

2 Many ships were sailing towards the island. (5)

3 The general praised the soldiers' bravery. (4)

4 I do not know the name of the boy. (3)

5 The old men were shouting in loud voices. (4)

Total: 20

Exercise 12.10

Translate the following into Latin:

1 Pupils are praised by wise masters. (5)

2 You are being punished, boy! (2)

3 Many weapons were being prepared by the Romans. (5)

4 The good girl was often praised by her mother. (5)

5 Many bodies were being carried. (3)

Total: 20

Exercise 12.11

Give the person, number, tense, mood, voice and the 1st person singular of the present indicative active of the following verbs:

1 miserat.

2 sciebat.

3 ibit.

4 possemus.

5 lusit.

6 perierunt.

7 nesciebamus.

8 poterat.

9 reguntur.

10 ostendet.

6 marks for each question. Total: 60

Exercise 12.12

Give the following verb parts:

1 The 1st person singular, imperfect subjunctive active of **fero**.

2 The 3rd person singular, imperfect subjunctive passive of **do**.

3 The 1st person plural, imperfect subjunctive active of **occido**.

4 The 2nd person singular, imperfect subjunctive passive of **paro**.

5 The 3rd person singular, imperfect subjunctive active of **volo**.

1 mark for each question. Total: 5

Exercise 12.13

Give and translate the following verb parts:

1 The 2nd person singular, imperfect indicative active of **scio**.

2 The 3rd person singular, perfect indicative active of **capio**.

3 The 3rd person plural, imperfect indicative active of **possum**.

4 The 3rd person plural, imperfect indicative active of **volo**.

5 The 3rd person plural, perfect indicative passive of **duco**.

6 The 1st person singular, future indicative active of **dico**.

7 The 3rd person plural, perfect indicative active of **facio**.

8 The 2nd person singular, perfect indicative active of **iacio**.

9 The 1st person plural, future indicative passive of **video**.

10 The 3rd person plural, perfect indicative active of **effugio**.

2 marks for each question. Total: 20

Exercise 12.14

Translate the following into Latin:

1 I know that the slave is hurrying.

2 I know that the slaves are hurrying.

3 I knew that the slave was hurrying.

4 I knew that the slaves were hurrying.

5 I hear that the woman is singing.

6 I hear that the women are singing.

7 I heard that the woman was singing.

8 I heard that the women were singing.

9 I see that the ships are coming.

10 I saw that the ships were coming.

3 marks for each question. Total: 30

Exercise 12.15

Translate the following into Latin:

1 All the pupils know that that teacher is wise. (7)

2 The king saw that the enemy were destroying the walls. (5)

3 The king saw that the walls were being destroyed by the enemy. (6)

4 The Romans knew that the Greeks were approaching quickly. (5)

5 We all knew that this old man could not walk. (7)

Total: 30

Exercise 12.16

Put into the plural and translate your answer:

1	hoc animal amo.	(3 + 3)
2	corpus magnum erat.	(3 + 3)
3	per viam longam iter facio.	(4 + 5)
4	scutum a milite portatum est.	(4 + 5)
5	magister superbus a discipulo non amabatur.	(4 + 6)

Total: 40

Exercise 12.17

Put into the singular and translate your answer:

1	naves mox advenerunt.	(2 + 3)
2	tandem duces militibus persuaserunt.	(3 + 4)
3	animalia per vias currebant.	(3 + 4)
4	senes milites crudeles timebant.	(4 + 4)
5	puellae a pueris saepe amantur.	(3 + 5)

Total: 35

Exercise 12.18

Translate the following into English:

1	quid cras faciemus?	(3)
2	multas horas dormiebam.	(3)
3	servos captos occiderunt.	(3)
4	multi libri ab eo scripti sunt.	(6)
5	dominus illorum servorum crudelissimus est.	(5)

Total: 20

Exercise 13.1

Translate the following passage. Line numbers are given on the left. New words are underlined in the text and their meanings given in the margin.

Odysseus hears that some of his men have been turned into pigs by the witch Circe on her island of Aeaea

1   Graeci ad insulam Aeaeam mox advenerunt.
    sex nautae in mediam insulam ab Ulixe missi
    sunt ut cibum aquamque peterent. multas horas
    afuerunt. tandem unus ex eis, Eurylochus
5   nomine, ad ceteros solus rediit. Graeci viderunt
    Eurylochum timere. Ulixes igitur Eurylocho
    imperavit ut quid accidisset statim narraret.   accidisset = had happened
    Eurylochus sic respondit: extra + acc. = outside

    'in media insula magnam domum invenimus, in
10 qua habitat dea pulcherrima, Circe nomine. illa
    nos domum intrare iussit ut vinum biberemus.'

    Eurylochus dixit se extra domum solum
    mansisse, sed ceteros intravisse et   mansisse = had stayed
    medicamentum a dea datum bibisse; dixit   intravisse = had entered
15 deam, baculum in manu tenentem, eos in   medicamentum, -i, n. = drug
    porcos mutavisse.   bibisse = had drunk
                                                     baculum, -i, n. = stick
    hoc audito Ulixes Eurylocho 'bene fecisti,'   manu = hand
    inquit. 'ego ad domum deae statim ibo ut eam   porcus, -i, m. = pig
    puniam comitesque nostros servem.' haec   mutavisse = had changed
20 verba locutus, Ulixes in mediam insulam   locutus = having spoken
    profectus est.   profectus est = set out

                                                     Total: 110

Exercise 13.2

1   From the passage give an example of:

    (a) a verb in the passive voice.   (1)

    (b) a relative pronoun.   (1)

    (c) a reflexive pronoun.   (1)

    (d) a present participle.   (1)

2   multas horas (line 3). In which case is this phrase? Why is this case used?   (2)

3   Eurylocho (line 6). In which case is this noun? Why is this case used?   (2)

4   ibo (line 18). Translate this word. Give the 1st person singular of the
    present indicative active of this verb.   (2)

                                                                    Total: 10

➔ Indirect statements: accusative and perfect infinitive

An indirect statement may refer to an action that took place in the past. In this case we use the accusative followed by the perfect infinitive.

Example

scio puellam venisse.	I know that the girl **has** come.
sciebam puellam venisse.	I knew that the girl **had** come.

Exercise 13.3

Translate the following into English:

1	audio nuntium advenisse.	(3)
2	audio nuntios advenisse.	(3)
3	audivi nuntium advenisse.	(3)
4	audivi nuntios advenisse.	(3)
5	scio illum puerum hoc fecisse.	(5)
6	scio illos pueros hoc fecisse.	(5)
7	sciebam puerum hoc fecisse.	(4)
8	sciebam pueros hoc fecisse.	(4)
9	sciebamus hos milites bene pugnavisse.	(5)
10	video Graecos tandem Troiam cepisse.	(5)

Total: 40

Exercise 13.4

Translate the following into English:

1	nuntius dicit hostes urbem cepisse.	(5)
2	nuntius dixit hostes urbem cepisse.	(5)
3	nuntius dicit urbem ab hostibus captam esse.	(7)
4	nuntius dixit urbem ab hostibus captam esse.	(7)
5	magister scit omnes discipulos bene laboravisse.	(6)
6	dux scit militem multa vulnera accepisse.	(6)
7	scio Romanos multas gentes vicisse.	(5)
8	audio te hunc librum legisse.	(5)
9	ille puer dixit se multos libros legisse.	(7)
10	scio hos milites fortiter tres dies pugnavisse.	(7)

Total: 60

Exercise 13.5

Translate the following into English:

1 nuntius dixit hostes tandem urbem delevisse. (6)

2 nuntius dixit urbem tandem ab hostibus deletam esse. (8)

3 dux sciebat milites multa vulnera accepisse. (6)

4 dux sciebat multa vulnera a militibus accepta esse. (8)

5 vidimus ancillam cenam bonam paravisse. (5)

6 vidimus cenam bonam ab ancilla paratam esse. (7)

7 sciebam illum dominum multos servos punivisse. (6)

8 sciebam multos servos ab illo domino punitos esse. (8)

9 magister dixit omnes discipulos hunc librum legisse. (7)

10 magister dixit hunc librum ab omnibus discipulis lectum esse. (9)

Total: 70

Exercise 13.6

Translate the following into English:

1 Graeci sciebant Helenam ad urbem Troiam a Paride ductam esse. (10)

2 Troiani viderunt Graecos multas naves paravisse. (6)

3 Graeci sciebant Troianos urbem bene defendisse. (6)

4 Graeci sciebant urbem a Troianis bene defensam esse. (8)

5 Troiani nesciebant Graecos equum ingentem aedificavisse. (6)

6 Troiani nesciebant equum ingentem a Graecis aedificatum esse. (8)

7 Graeci sciebant se Troianos vicisse. (5)

8 Troiani sciebant se a Graecis victos esse. (7)

9 cives viderunt Graecos multa templa delevisse. (6)

10 cives viderunt multa templa a Graecis deleta esse. (8)

Total: 70

➡ How to translate infinitives: a reminder

main verb	+ infinitive	translate infinitive as	example
present	present	is, are	scio puellam venire.
			I know that the girl is coming.
past	present	was, were	sciebam puellam venire.
			I knew that the girl was coming.
present	perfect	has, have	scio puellam venisse.
			I know that the girl has come.
past	perfect	had	sciebam puellam venisse.
			I knew that the girl had come.

Exercise 13.7

Translate the following into English:

1 Ulixes sciebat se uxorem suam diu non vidisse. (8)

2 Polyphemus vidit Graecos cibum suum cepisse. (6)

3 Graeci sciebant se a Polyphemo conspectos esse. (7)

4 comites Ulixis sciebant se malos fuisse. (6)

5 Graeci viderunt Eurylochum timere. (4)

6 Eurylochus dixit se deam pulcherrimam in media insula vidisse. (9)

7 Eurylochus dixit deam in magna villa habitare. (7)

8 Eurylochus dixit se deam timuisse. (5)

9 Troiani viderunt exercitum Graecorum magnum esse. (6)

10 Graeci credebant se Troiam capere non posse. (7)

Total: 65

Exercise 13.8

Translate the following into English:

1 dux vidit oppidum a Romanis oppugnari. (6)

2 vir dixit se multas feminas pulchras amavisse. (7)

3 vir dixit multas feminas pulchras a se amatas esse. (9)

4 audio hunc librum longissimum esse. (5)

5 vidimus multos equos ex agro currere. (6)

6 milites viderunt hostes celeriter appropinquare. (5)

7 dux sciebat urbem ab hostibus captam esse. (7)

8 audio Graecos Troiam cepisse. (4)

9 scio te hunc librum legere velle. (6)

10 nuntius nuntiavit Romanos pugnare nolle. (5)

Total: 60

Exercise 13.9

Translate the following into English:

1 scio me discipulum optimum esse. (5)

2 puella dixit se timere. (4)

3 puellae dixerunt se timere. (4)

4 Iulius Caesar sciebat se ducem bonum esse. (7)

5 puella sciebat se pulchram esse. (5)

6 milites dixerunt se pugnare velle. (5)

7 omnes puellae sciunt se meliores quam pueros esse. (8)

8 regina credebat se mulierem pulcherrimam esse. (6)

9 Menelaus nuntiavit se Troianos punire cupere. (6)

10 Polyphemus dixit se vinum amare. (5)

Total: 55

→ Revision

Exercise 13.10

Translate the following into Latin:

1 The wise old men fled from the city. (5)

2 The parents of the girl were afraid. (3)

3 We defeated the enemy because of our bravery. (4)

4 The slaves were carrying dead bodies. (4)

5 We all like easy tasks. (4)

Total: 20

Exercise 13.11

Translate the following into Latin:

1 Messengers were sent to the city. (4)

2 Spears were thrown across the road. (4)

3 The wicked king was defeated by the enemy. (5)

4 Many weapons were being collected by the citizens. (5)

5 The old man was killed. (2)

Total: 20

Exercise 13.12

Translate the following into Latin:

1 I know that the pupil has worked well. (4)

2 I know that the pupils have worked well. (4)

3 I knew that the pupil had worked well. (4)

4 I knew that the pupils had worked well. (4)

5 We see that the ship has arrived. (3)

6 We see that the ships have arrived. (3)

7 We saw that the ship had arrived. (3)

8 We saw that the ships had arrived. (3)

9 He heard that the girl had hurried. (3)

10 We did not know that the city had already been captured. (4)

Total: 35

Exercise 13.13

Translate the following into Latin:

1 The soldiers knew that the storm had destroyed the ships. (5)

2 The messenger announced that the army had been defeated. (4)

3 The sailors know that the ship has sailed out of the harbour. (6)

4 The general saw that many soldiers had been wounded. (5)

5 We heard that the enemy had killed all the citizens. (5)

Total: 25

Exercise 13.14

Give the person, number, tense, mood, voice and the 1st person singular of the present indicative active of the following verbs:

1 fuit.   6 vicit.

2 adiret.   7 aedificabatur.

3 nolueram.   8 essent.

4 conspexerunt.   9 credebat.

5 scribebamus.   10 stabamus.

6 marks for each question. Total: 60

Exercise 13.15

Give the following verb parts:

1 The 1st person plural, imperfect subjunctive active of iacio.

2 The 3rd person plural, imperfect subjunctive passive of iubeo.

3 The 1st person singular, imperfect subjunctive active of eo.

4 The 2nd person plural, imperfect subjunctive passive of laudo.

5 The 3rd person singular, imperfect subjunctive active of sum.

1 mark for each question. Total: 5

Exercise 13.16

Give and translate the following verb parts:

1 The 3rd person singular, perfect indicative active of **nuntio**.

2 The 3rd person singular, perfect indicative passive of **occido**.

3 The 1st person plural, pluperfect indicative active of **oppugno**.

4 The 3rd person plural, perfect indicative active of **pello**.

5 The 3rd person singular, imperfect indicative passive of **fero**.

6 The 3rd person plural, perfect indicative active of **possum**.

7 The 1st person plural, future indicative passive of **moveo**.

8 The 3rd person plural, perfect indicative active of **mitto**.

9 The 3rd person singular, future indicative passive of **libero**.

10 The 1st person plural, imperfect indicative active of **rogo**.

2 marks for each question. Total: 20

Exercise 13.17

Translate the following into English:

1 dominus quem servus timebat crudelis erat. (6)

2 servus fugiebat quod dominum timebat. (5)

3 dux milites urbem statim occupare iussit. (6)

4 servi ab eo saepe puniebantur. (5)

5 in urbem itis. (3)

Total: 25

Exercise 14.1

Translate the following passage. Line numbers are given on the left. New words are underlined in the text and their meanings given in the margin.

Odysseus meets Circe

1 Ulixes, <u>cum</u> verba Eurylochi <u>audivisset</u>, in
mediam insulam <u>profectus est</u> ut comites
servaret et <u>Circen</u> puniret. Eurylochus territus
Ulixem <u>sequi</u> nolebat. Ulixes domum deae mox
5 invenit. domum <u>ingressus</u>, <u>cum</u> ad deam
<u>appropinquavisset</u>, haec verba ei <u>locutus est</u>:

'dea mala es, Circe. scio te comites meos in
<u>porcos</u> <u>mutavisse</u>.' Circe, his verbis auditis,
Ulixi respondit: 'noli iratus esse, Ulixes. cape
10 hoc vinum.' <u>medicamentum</u> Ulixi dare <u>conata
est</u>, sed frustra: nam ille a deis <u>protegebatur</u>.
Circe timebat. <u>cum</u> sciret se Ulixem in <u>porcum
mutare</u> non posse, clamavit: 'vir felix es,
Ulixes. a deis <u>protegeris</u>. ego comites tuos in
15 <u>formam</u> <u>humanam</u> statim <u>revertam</u>.' haec verba
<u>locuta</u> Circe Graecos <u>hortata est</u> ut secum diu
manerent. Graeci in insula <u>Circes</u> unum annum
manserunt.

cum = when
audivisset = had heard
profectus est = set off
Circen = accusative of
Circe (Greek form)
sequi = to follow
ingressus = having entered
appropinquavisset = (he)
had approached
locutus est = he spoke
porcus, -i, m. = pig
muto, -are, - avi, -atum (1)
= I change
medicamentum, -i n. =
drug
conata est = she tried
protego, -ere, -tegi,
-tectum (3) = I protect
cum = since
forma, -ae, f. = shape
humanus, -a, -um = human
reverto, -ere, -verti,
-versum (3) = I turn back
locuta = having spoken
hortata est = she
encouraged
Circes = genitive of Circe
(Greek form)

Total: 90

Exercise 14.2

1 From the passage give an example of:

   (a) a verb in the imperfect subjunctive. (1)

   (b) a reflexive pronoun. (1)

2 ei (line 6). In which case is this pronoun? (1)

3 unum annum (line 17). In which case is this phrase? Why is this case used? (2)

Total: 5

→ Deponent verbs

Deponent verbs are passive in form but active in meaning.

	normal passive verb		deponent verb	
present	amor	I am loved	conor	I try
infinitive	amari	to be loved	conari	to try
perfect	amatus sum	I was loved	conatus sum	I tried
future	amabor	I will be loved	conabor	I will try
imperfect	amabar	I was being loved	conabar	I was trying
pluperfect	amatus eram	I had been loved	conatus eram	I had tried

Now would be a good time to revise the passive endings of the different verb conjugations. Have a copy of these in front of you as you tackle the exercises which follow.

Exercises 14.3–14.17

Translate the verb forms into English. (1 mark for each question. Total: 150.)

Exercise 14.3

1 conatur.

2 ingrederis.

3 proficiscimur.

4 loquor.

5 sequuntur.

6 hortatur.

7 conamur.

8 loquuntur.

9 conantur.

10 ingrediuntur.

Exercise 14.4

1 conaris.

2 proficiscitur.

3 hortamini.

4 conor.

5 ingreditur.

6 hortamur.

7 loquitur.

8 conamini.

9 proficiscimini.

10 sequor.

Exercise 14.5

1 ingredimini.

2 hortaris.

3 loquimini.

4 profisceris.

5 loqueris.

6 sequimini.

7 proficiscor.

8 ingredimur.

9 hortantur.

10 ingredior.

Exercise 14.6

1 sequebatur.

2 ingrediebar.

3 loquebar.

4 hortabar.

5 conabamur.

6 proficiscebamur.

7 hortabamur.

8 ingrediebatur.

9 sequebantur.

10 loquebatur.

Exercise 14.7

1 conabamini.

2 sequebar.

3 ingrediebaris.

4 loquebantur.

5 conabatur.

6 proficiscebaris.

7 hortabamini.

8 loquebamini.

9 ingrediebamur.

10 hortabatur.

Exercise 14.8

1 hortabaris.

2 ingrediebantur.

3 conabantur.

4 proficiscebatur.

5 sequebaris.

6 ingrediebamini.

7 hortabantur.

8 proficiscebar.

9 conabaris.

10 loquebamur.

Exercise 14.9

1 ingredietur.

2 sequentur.

3 hortabimur.

4 ingrediemini.

5 loquar.

6 conabor.

7 sequetur.

8 proficiscetur.

9 hortabuntur.

10 conabuntur.

Exercise 14.10

1 loquemini.

2 conabimur.

3 proficiscentur.

4 loquentur.

5 hortabitur.

6 loqueris.

7 ingrediemur.

8 conaberis.

9 loquemur.

10 sequeris.

Exercise 14.11

1 conabimini.
2 sequemini.
3 hortabimini.
4 ingredientur.
5 sequemur.

6 conabitur.
7 loquetur.
8 proficisceris.
9 hortabor.
10 proficiscar.

Exercise 14.12

1 sequimur.
2 sequemur.
3 ingrediemur.
4 conabantur.
5 hortabantur.

6 ingredimur.
7 conabaris.
8 ingredientur.
9 sequitur.
10 proficiscebatur.

Exercise 14.13

1 ingrediebamini.
2 proficisceris.
3 conabimini.
4 proficiscuntur.
5 hortantur.

6 hortabimini.
7 ingredimini.
8 ingrediebantur.
9 conabitur.
10 loquebamur.

Exercise 14.14

1 proficiscor.
2 sequebaris.
3 loquimini.
4 sequemini.
5 hortor.

6 proficiscebar.
7 sequimini.
8 loquetur.
9 loquimur.
10 proficiscar.

Exercise 14.15

1 conatus est.
2 conata est.
3 conatus erat.
4 conata erat.
5 conati sunt.

6 conati erant.
7 secuti erant.
8 locuta est.
9 profecti erant.
10 ingressi estis.

Exercise 14.16

1 hortatus es.	6 profecta est.
2 secuti estis.	7 hortatus erat.
3 ingressa est.	8 secutus est.
4 locuti sumus.	9 profecti sumus.
5 profectus est.	10 locuti sunt.

Exercise 14.17

1 ingressus est.	6 locutus est.
2 locuta erat.	7 secuti eratis.
3 profecti sunt.	8 ingressi sumus.
4 locutus erat.	9 ingressa erat.
5 ingressi eratis.	10 hortata est.

1 mark for each question. Total: 150

Exercise 14.18

Translate the following into English:

1 dux bonus milites suos semper hortatur. (6)

2 hoc facere cras conabor. (4)

3 rex multa verba civibus locutus est. (6)

4 servi in villam ingressi sunt. (5)

5 pater haec verba locutus est, deinde discessit. (7)

6 mater filium hortata est ut bene laboraret. (7)

7 servi ex urbe effugere conati sunt. (6)

8 ille puer hanc puellam sequebatur. (5)

9 milites ex oppido capto profecti sunt. (6)

10 rex cives hortatus est ut urbem fortiter defenderent. (8)

Total: 60

Exercise 14.19

Translate the following into English:

1 Menelaus ad urbem Troiam profectus est. (6)

2 multae naves eum secutae sunt. (5)

3 Graeci Troiam celeriter capere conati sunt. (6)

4 Graeci in urbem Troiam tandem ingressi sunt. (7)

5 Agamemnon Graecos hortatus est ut bene pugnarent. (7)

6 dux multa verba amicis locutus est. (6)

7 dux amicos hortatus est ut naves pararent. (7)

8 dux comitesque ex urbe Troia profecti sunt. (8)

9 Graeci domum redire conabantur. (4)

10 Graeci mox proficisci cupiebant. (4)

Total: 60

Exercise 14.20

Translate the following into English:

1 cur loquimini, pueri? laborate! (4)

2 noli loqui, puer. labora! (4)

3 dux milites cras hortabitur. (4)

4 servi in templum effugere conabantur. (5)

5 dominus tamen servos sequebatur. (4)

6 ex urbe heri profecti sumus. (5)

7 naves e portu celeriter profectae sunt. (6)

8 magister discipulis imperavit ne loquerentur. (5)

9 scio omnes puellas loqui amare. (5)

10 audio omnes naves e portu iam profectas esse. (8)

Total: 50

Exercise 14.21

Translate the following into English:

1 dux civibus persuasit ut se sequerentur. (6)

2 dominus servo imperavit ut in villam ingrederetur. (7)

3 hunc ducem sequi nolo. (4)

4 nolite loqui, discipuli! me audite! (5)

5 hic puer laborare numquam conatur. (5)

6 Menelaus Graecos hortatus est ut ad urbem statim proficiscerentur. (9)

7 Graeci ex urbe mox proficisci volebant. (6)

8 viri mortui numquam loquuntur. (4)

9 naves Graecorum e portu sine mora profectae erant. (8)

10 milites in oppidum mox ingressi sunt. (6)

Total: 60

Exercise 14.22

Translate the following into Latin:

1 The enemy crossed the river. (3)

2 The brave soldiers sailed across the sea. (5)

3 We are listening to the master's wise words. (4)

4 Generals praise bravery. (3)

5 The big storm destroyed many ships. (5)

Total: 20

Exercise 14.23

Translate the following into Latin:

1 Wise pupils are praised by teachers. (5)

2 A body was found on the ship. (4)

3 The master was being defended by the brave slave. (5)

4 The young man used to be praised. (2)

5 Many rewards were given to the soldiers. (4)

Total: 20

Exercise 14.24

Translate the following into Latin:

1 We set out.

2 I go in.

3 We are following.

4 I was encouraging.

5 We try.

6 They are following.

7 You (sing.) will enter.

8 I am setting out.

9 He is speaking.

10 They were speaking.

1 mark for each question. Total: 10

Exercise 14.25

Translate the following into Latin:

1 I am trying.

2 We will encourage.

3 She was speaking.

4 You (pl.) will follow.

5 They were setting out.

6 We enter.

7 I will follow.

8 They were following.

9 They are speaking.

10 He encourages.

1 mark for each question. Total: 10

Exercise 14.26

Translate the following into Latin:

1 He set out.
2 She set out.
3 They set out.
4 We encouraged.
5 I tried.

6 They spoke.
7 She spoke.
8 You (sing.) followed.
9 He entered.
10 You (pl.) encouraged.

1 mark for each question. Total: 10

Exercise 14.27

Translate the following into Latin:

1 They had tried.
2 He had spoken.
3 She had spoken.
4 We had entered.
5 They had set out.

6 You (pl.) had encouraged.
7 I had followed.
8 You (sing.) had entered.
9 She had tried.
10 He had encouraged.

1 mark for each question. Total: 10

Exercise 14.28

Translate the following into Latin:

1 The leader's ships will set out from the harbour tomorrow.
2 Good pupils always try to work well.
3 The soldiers set out from the city at the second hour.
4 Good generals always want to encourage their soldiers.
5 The enemy entered the city suddenly in the middle of the night.

6 marks for each question. Total: 30

Exercise 14.29

Translate the following into Latin:

1 The general will encourage his soldiers to fight well. (6)
2 The sailors wanted to set out from the harbour immediately. (6)
3 I am going into this villa. Do not follow me! (7)
4 Many very brave men had tried to cross this river, but in vain. (10)
5 We know that that teacher always encourages his pupils. (6)

Total: 35

Exercise 14.30

Give the following verb parts:

1 The 1st person plural, imperfect subjunctive active of **convenio**.

2 The 1st person plural, imperfect subjunctive passive of **vinco**.

3 The 3rd person singular, imperfect subjunctive active of **supero**.

4 The 2nd person plural, imperfect subjunctive passive of **capio**.

5 The 1st person plural, imperfect subjunctive active of **pugno**.

1 mark for each question. Total: 5

Exercise 14.31

Give and translate the following verb parts:

1 The 3rd person singular, imperfect indicative active of **nescio**.

2 The 3rd person singular, perfect indicative deponent of **conor**.

3 The 3rd person plural, present indicative deponent of **loquor**.

4 The 1st person singular, perfect indicative deponent of **sequor**.

5 The 1st person plural, imperfect indicative active of **habito**.

6 The 3rd person singular, future indicative passive of **invenio**.

7 The 3rd person singular, imperfect indicative passive of **lego**.

8 The 3rd person plural, perfect indicative active of **scribo**.

9 The 2nd person singular, pluperfect indicative active of **facio**.

10 The 3rd person singular, future indicative active of **eo**.

2 marks for each question. Total: 20

Exercise 14.32

Give the person, number, tense, mood, voice and the 1st person singular of the present indicative active of the following verbs:

1 potes.

2 sciemus.

3 dabatur.

4 dixit.

5 exierunt.

6 fugeret.

7 habebimus.

8 habitabamus.

9 navigat.

10 posueram.

6 marks for each question. Total: 60

Exercise 14.33

Put into the plural and translate your answer:

1 mulier pecuniam amat. (3 + 3)
2 puella loquitur. (2 + 2)
3 senex ambulare conatus est. (3 + 3)
4 mater filiam secuta est. (3 + 3)
5 exercitus in urbe erat. (4 + 4)

Total: 30

Exercise 14.34

Put into the singular and translate your answer:

1 animalia saeva effugerunt. (3 + 3)
2 nautae proficiscuntur. (2 + 2)
3 duces milites hortabantur. (3 + 3)
4 custodes servos secuti sunt. (3 + 3)
5 naves ex insulis profectae sunt. (4 + 4)

Total: 30

Exercise 14.35

Translate the following into English:

1 nemo sapientior est quam ego. (5)
2 hic est servus bonus cui cibum dedi. (7)
3 urbem captam delevimus. (3)
4 noli clamare! laborare conamur. (4)
5 illa via longior est quam haec. (6)

Total: 25

Exercise 15.1

Translate the following passage. Line numbers are given on the left. New words are underlined in the text and their meanings given in the margin.

Odysseus and Calypso

1 Graeci, <u>cum</u> in insula <u>Circes</u> unum annum
   <u>mansissent</u>, proficisci tandem constituerunt ut
   domum redirent <u>familias</u>que iterum viderent.
   <u>cum</u> trans mare navigarent multa <u>monstra</u>
5 viderunt, multa pericula <u>subierunt</u>, multa mala
   <u>passi sunt</u>. tandem omnes Graeci, <u>praeter</u>
   Ulixem ipsum, <u>aut</u> interfecti <u>aut</u> <u>mortui</u> erant.
   Ulixes ipse, undis et ventis <u>actus</u>, ad insulam
   Ogygiam, ubi habitabat <u>nympha</u> pulchra
10 Calypso, tandem advenit. Calypso, <u>cum</u> Ulixem
   <u>vidisset</u>, eum magnopere amavit et ei <u>nubere</u>
   cupiebat. ille tamen, <u>cum</u> uxorem suam amaret
   domumque redire cuperet, noluit. Calypso
   Ulixem in insula septem annos tenuit. tandem,
15 a dis iussa, <u>rate</u> facta, Ulixem ab insula sua
   discedere <u>sivit</u>.

cum = when
Circes = genitive of Circe
(Greek form)
mansissent = had stayed
familia, -ae, f. = family
cum + imperfect
subjunctive = while, since
monstrum, -i, n. = monster
subeo, subire, subii =
I undergo
patior, pati, passus sum
(3½) = I suffer
praeter + acc. = except for
aut … aut … = either … or …
morior, mori, mortuus
sum (3½) = I die
ago, -ere, egi, actum (3)
= I drive
nympha, -ae, f. = nymph
vidisset = had seen
nubo, -ere, nupsi, nuptum
+dat. (3) = I marry
rates, -is, f. = raft
sino, -ere, sivi, situm (3)
= I allow

Total: 80

Exercise 15.2

1 From the passage give an example of:

   (a) a deponent verb. (1)

   (b) a past participle passive. (1)

   (c) an infinitive. (1)

2 redirent (line 3). In which mood is this verb? (1)

3 mare (line 4). In which case is this noun? Why is this case used? (2)

4 noluit (line 13). Give the person, number, tense and the 1st person
   singular of the present indicative active of this verb. (4)

Total: 10

→ cum + pluperfect subjunctive

Example

servus, **cum** reginam **vidisset**, laetus erat.

When the slave **had** seen the queen, he was happy.

Exercise 15.3

Translate the following into English:

1 pueri, cum magistrum vidissent, fugerunt. (5)

2 magister, cum puerum punivisset, risit. (5)

3 milites, cum multos viros occidissent, urbem ceperunt. (7)

4 pueri, cum in villam iniissent, matrem audiverunt. (7)

5 Romani, cum urbem cepissent, eam deleverunt. (6)

6 poeta, cum librum scripsisset, laetus erat. (6)

7 servi, cum opus fecissent, laeti erant. (6)

8 milites, cum bene pugnavissent, multa praemia acceperunt. (7)

9 milites, cum hostes vidissent, timebant. (5)

10 cum Romani hostes conspexissent, statim oppugnaverunt. (6)

Total: 60

Exercise 15.4

Translate the following into English:

1 Paris, cum Helenam visam amavisset, eam statim cepit. (8)

2 Menelaus, cum Paris Helenam cepisset, iratus erat. (7)

3 milites, cum omnia paravissent, profecti sunt. (6)

4 Graeci, cum magnas copias paravissent, ad urbem Troiam navigaverunt. (9)

5 Graeci, cum ad urbem Troiam navigavissent, muros oppugnaverunt. (8)

6 Graeci, cum urbem decem annos oppugnavissent, tandem equum ingentem fecerunt. (10)

7 Graeci, cum equum ingentem fecissent, eum prope urbem reliquerunt. (9)

8 cives, cum equum conspexissent, eum in urbem duxerunt. (8)

9 cives, cum equum in urbem duxissent, laeti erant. (8)

10 Graeci, cum Troiam delevissent, ad Graeciam redierunt. (7)

Total: 80

97

→ cum + imperfect subjunctive

Examples

servi, **cum laborarent**, dominum viderunt.
While/When the slaves were working, they saw the master.

servi, **cum** fessi **essent**, bene non laborabant.
Since the slaves were tired, they were not working well.

Exercise 15.5

Translate the following into English:

1	agricola, cum in agris laboraret, multos equos vidit.	(8)
2	milites, cum fessi essent, non bene pugnaverunt.	(7)
3	dux, cum dormiret, a servo occisus est.	(7)
4	milites, cum hostes timerent, pugnare nolebant.	(6)
5	multae naves, cum ad insulam navigarent, tempestate deletae sunt.	(9)
6	dominus, cum servum non amaret, eum interfecit.	(7)
7	milites audaces, cum fortiter pugnarent, multa vulnera acceperunt.	(8)
8	multi cives, cum urbs ab hostibus oppugnaretur, effugerunt.	(8)
9	pueri, cum magistrum crudelem non amarent, non laborabant.	(8)
10	magister, cum puer non laboraret, iratus erat.	(7)

Total: 75

Exercise 15.6

Translate the following into English:

1	magister, cum iratus esset, puerum punivit.	(6)
2	cum magister puerum punivisset, puer tristis erat.	(7)
3	puer, cum tristis esset, flevit.	(5)
4	cum puer fleret, mater eius irata erat.	(7)
5	mater pueri, cum irata esset, ad magistrum festinavit.	(8)
6	magister, cum mater pueri irata esset, timebat.	(7)
7	magister, cum perterritus esset, statim fugit.	(6)
8	pueri, cum magister fugisset, non laboraverunt.	(6)
9	cum servus celeriter curreret, nemo eum capere poterat.	(8)
10	dea, cum sciret se Ulixem interficere non posse, irata erat.	(10)

Total: 70

 **Revision**

Exercise 15.7

Translate the following into Latin:

1 We do not like work. (3)

2 The soldiers killed many animals in the woods. (6)

3 I did not like the queen's voice. (4)

4 The cruel parents frightened the boy. (4)

5 We are fighting for our country. (3)

Total: 20

Exercise 15.8

Translate the following into Latin:

1 The old man was left in the city. (4)

2 The ships are destroyed by the storm. (3)

3 Many javelins were thrown by the brave soldiers. (6)

4 The master's money was being guarded by soldiers. (5)

5 The gods are praised. (2)

Total: 20

Exercise 15.9

Translate the following into Latin:

1 When the sailors had prepared the ship, they set out. (5)

2 When the soldiers had destroyed the city, they departed. (5)

3 When the pupils had heard the teacher's words, they were happy. (7)

4 When the old man had seen the beautiful girl, he smiled. (6)

5 When the girls had run for many hours, they were tired. (7)

Total: 30

Exercise 15.10

Translate the following into Latin:

1 Since the soldiers were brave, they fought well. (6)

2 While we were sailing, we saw many ships. (5)

3 Since the master was cruel, he used to punish his slaves. (6)

4 While I was walking along the road, I saw a beautiful girl. (7)

5 While the farmers were working, they saw many animals. (6)

Total: 30

Exercise 15.11

Give the following verb parts:

1 The 1st person singular, pluperfect subjunctive active of **sum**.

2 The 3rd person plural, pluperfect subjunctive passive of **porto**.

3 The 3rd person singular, pluperfect subjunctive active of **do**.

4 The 2nd person singular, imperfect subjunctive active of **possum**.

5 The 3rd person singular, imperfect subjunctive passive of **defendo**.

1 mark for each question. Total: 5

Exercise 15.12

Give the person, number, tense, mood, voice and the 1st person singular of the present indicative active of the following verbs:

1 regitur.   6 vocaverunt.

2 timeret.   7 tradidit.

3 vidisset.   8 staret.

4 spectabatur.   9 sedebamus.

5 miseramus.   10 scripsit.

6 marks for each question. Total: 60

Exercise 15.13

Give and translate the following verb parts:

1 The 3rd person plural, perfect indicative active of **discedo**.

2 The 1st person singular, future indicative active of **curro**.

3 The 1st person plural, future indicative active of **possum**.

4 The 1st person singular, perfect indicative active of **fero**.

5 The 3rd person singular, perfect indicative deponent of **morior**.

6 The present infinitive deponent of **patior**.

7 The 1st person plural, imperfect indicative passive of **amo**.

8 The 3rd person plural, future indicative active of **volo**.

9 The plural imperative of **eo**.

10 The 2nd person singular, imperfect indicative active of **nolo**.

2 marks for each question. Total: 20

Exercise 15.14

Translate the following into English:

1 cur pater meus ad murum it?   (6)

2 pecuniam omnes magnopere amamus.   (4)

3 pueri ex agris in villam cucurrerunt.   (6)

4 dominus servum occidit quod numquam bene laborabat.   (7)

5 servus miser a domino crudeli occisus est.   (7)

Total: 30

Exercise 16.1

Translate the following passage. Line numbers are given on the left. New words are underlined in the text and their meanings given in the margin.

The Phaeacians

1 Ulixes, ubi ab insula Ogygia profectus est,
   multos dies in <u>rate</u> <u>progressus</u>, ad insulam
   <u>Phaeacum</u> – quorum rex Alcinous erat –
   tandem pulsus est. Alcinous, cum aurum
5 multaque dona ei dedisset, tandem eum rogavit
   quis esset. Ulixes <u>explicavit</u> se Ulixem esse; se
   exercitumque suum Troiam cepisse; comites
   suos omnes <u>aut</u> mortuos <u>aut</u> interfectos esse;
   se uxorem filiumque iterum videre cupere.

10 Phaeaces, verbis Ulixis auditis, eum hortati sunt
   ne timeret. donis in navem positis, Ulixem ad
   insulam Ithacam <u>celeritate</u> <u>magica</u> tulerunt.
   Ulixes, e nave <u>egressus</u>, in patria sua tandem
   stabat.

rates, -is, f. = raft
progressus = having gone on
Phaeaces, -um, m. pl. = the Phaeacians

explico, -are, -avi, -atum (1) = I explain
aut ... aut ... = either ... or ...

celeritas, -tatis, f. = speed
magicus, -a, -um = magical
egressus = having got off

Total: 75

Exercise 16.2

1 From the passage give an example of:

   (a) a relative pronoun.   (1)

   (b) a pluperfect subjunctive.

   (c) a reflexive pronoun.   (1)

   (d) an ablative absolute.   (1)

   (e) a perfect infinitive.   (1)

2 multos dies (line 2). In which case is this phrase? Why is this case used? (2)

3 celeritate magica (line 12). In which case is this phrase?   (1)

4 tulerunt (line 12). In which tense is this verb? Give the 1st person singular of
   the present indicative active of this verb.   (2)

Total: 10

→ Perfect deponent participles

> **Reminder:** although passive in form, deponents are active in meaning:
>
> conor, conari, conatus sum (1), I try   conatus = having tried
>
> loquor, loqui, locutus sum (3), I speak   locutus = having spoken
>
> proficiscor, proficisci, profectus sum (3), I set out   profectus = having set out

Example

dux, haec verba locutus, discessit.

The general, **having spoken** these words, departed.

or

The general **spoke** these words **and** departed.

Exercise 16.3

Translate the following into English:

1 servus fessus, effugere conatus, a domino captus est.   (8)

2 puellae, prima luce profectae, ad urbem mox advenerunt.   (8)

3 dux audax, milites suos hortatus, in proelium ruit.   (8)

4 puer, in villam ingressus, amicum vidit.   (6)

5 puella, in villam ingressa, amicum vidit.   (6)

6 miles, multa vulnera passus, mortuus est.   (6)

7 nautae, multos dies progressi, ad insulam tandem pulsi sunt.   (9)

8 miles fortis, in illo proelio mortuus, a comitibus laudatus est.   (10)

9 servi, e templo egressi, domum festinaverunt.   (6)

10 milites, ducem diu secuti, contra hostes tandem pugnaverunt.   (8)

Total: 75

Exercise 16.4

Translate the following into English:

1 milites Graeci, e Graecia profecti, ad urbem Troiam navigaverunt.   (9)

2 Menelaus, omnes Graecos hortatus, eos naves parare iussit.   (8)

3 naves Graecorum, multos dies progressae, ad urbem Troiam tandem advenerunt.   (11)

4 Graeci, Troiam multos annos capere conati, equum ingentem in litore aedificare constituerunt.   (11)

5 Graeci, ex equo egressi, multos Troianos occiderunt.   (7)

6 cives, multa vulnera passi, a Graecis occisi sunt. (8)

7 rex, Troianos hortatus ut arma colligerent, contra Graecos ruit. (9)

8 ceteri Graeci, in urbem ingressi, multos Troianos interfecerunt. (8)

9 naves, e portu profectae, ad urbem Troiam mox advenerunt. (9)

10 multi Troiani, in proelio mortui, ab omnibus civibus laudati sunt. (10)

Total: 90

→ Revision

Exercise 16.5

Translate the following into Latin:

1 Having spoken these words, the man left. (5)

2 Having spoken these words, the woman left. (5)

3 Having set out immediately, the ship soon arrived. (5)

4 Having encouraged the soldiers, the general advanced. (4)

5 Having tried to fight well, the Romans were however beaten. (6)

Total: 25

Exercise 16.6

Translate the following into Latin:

1 Having suffered many wounds, the queen died. (5)

2 Having followed the enemy across the mountains, the Romans immediately attacked. (7)

3 Having entered the villa, the young man saw many friends. (6)

4 Having advanced to the river, the general encouraged the soldiers. (6)

5 Having left the town, the slaves ran into the fields. (6)

Total: 30

Exercise 16.7

Put into the plural and translate your answer:

1 vir mulierem diu spectabat. (3 + 4)

2 miles fortis murum oppugnavit. (4 + 4)

3 puer illam puellam iam conspexerat. (4 + 5)

4 hominem mortuum in via vidi. (4 + 5)

5 navis ad portum pellebatur. (3 + 4)

Total: 40

Chapter 16

Exercise 16.8

Put into the singular and translate your answer:

1 dona saepe accipimus.   (2 + 3)

2 senes pugnare noluerunt.   (3 + 3)

3 cives oppida bene defendebant.   (3 + 4)

4 milites a servis custodiebantur.   (3 + 4)

5 scuta a pueris saepe ferebantur.   (4 + 6)

Total: 35

Exercise 16.9

Give the following verb parts:

1 The 3rd person plural, pluperfect subjunctive active of eo.

2 The 3rd person singular, pluperfect subjunctive passive of voco.

3 The 1st person singular, pluperfect subjunctive active of maneo.

4 The 2nd person singular, imperfect subjunctive active of scribo.

5 The 3rd person plural, imperfect subjunctive passive of rego.

1 mark for each question. Total: 5

Exercise 16.10

Give and translate the following verb parts:

1 The 3rd person singular, present indicative deponent of progredior.

2 The 3rd person plural, perfect indicative active of do.

3 The 3rd person plural, imperfect indicative passive of dico.

4 The 3rd person plural, perfect indicative active of exeo.

5 The 2nd person singular, present indicative active of possum.

6 The 1st person plural, pluperfect indicative active of video.

7 The 2nd person plural, imperfect indicative active of venio.

8 The 3rd person singular, perfect indicative active of iubeo.

9 The 3rd person singular, imperfect indicative passive of moveo.

10 The 1st person plural, future indicative active of navigo.

2 marks for each question. Total: 20

Exercise 16.11

Give the person, number, tense, mood, voice and the 1st person singular of the present indicative active of the following verbs:

1	fui.	6	posuerat.
2	movisset.	7	tulerunt.
3	timebant.	8	amatus erat.
4	ibis.	9	esses.
5	constituerat.	10	nolebamus.

6 marks for each question. Total: 60

Exercise 16.12

Translate the following into English:

1 ludere hodie non possum. (4)

2 hoc facto, omnes feminae statim discesserunt. (6)

3 equus maximus a Graecis factus est. (6)

4 nomen huius puellae Cornelia est. (5)

5 ille vir clarus est. filii eius clari quoque sunt. (9)

Total: 30

Exercise 16.13

Translate the following into Latin:

1 The soldiers collected many weapons. (4)

2 We have a dear mother. (3)

3 You (sing.) were standing in the middle of the city. (4)

4 We heard the enemy's shouts. (3)

5 The big crowd was running towards the temples of the gods. (6)

Total: 20

Exercise 16.14

Translate the following into Latin:

1 Many long roads were built by the Romans. (6)

2 Money was found in the road by the lucky slave. (7)

3 The slaves are being punished. (2)

4 The Greeks were beaten. (2)

5 A bright light was seen. (3)

Total: 20

(End of Common Academic Scholarship prescription)

17

Exercise 17.1

Translate the following passage. Line numbers are given on the left. New words are underlined in the text and their meanings given in the margin.

Penelope's problems

1 Troia capta, principes Graecorum ad patrias
suas iam redierant. in insula Ithaca autem
Penelope, uxor Ulixis, quod coniugem suum
multos annos non viderat, tam tristis erat ut
5 saepe fleret. multi viri nobiles interea ad regiam
Penelopes venerant. hi credebant Ulixem
mortuum esse; illum numquam domum
rediturum esse. putabant Penelopen coniugem
suum numquam iterum visuram esse. omnes
10 Penelopen – mulierem pulchram et divitem – in
matrimonium ducere cupiebant. Penelope
autem coniugem novum eligere noluit. sperabat
enim Ulixem ad Ithacam mox adventurum esse,
procosque tum a regia sua discessuros esse.
15 nesciebat Penelope Ulixem in insula Ithaca iam
adesse.

tam = so
regia, -ae, f. = palace
Penelopes = genitive of
Penelope (Greek form)
rediturum esse = would
return
puto, -are, -avi, -atum (1)
= I think
visuram esse = would see
dives, divitis = rich
in matrimonium ducere =
to marry
eligo, -ere, elegi, electum
(3) = I select, choose
spero, -are, -avi, -atum (1)
= I hope
enim = for
adventurum esse = would
arrive
procus, -i, m. = suitor
discessuros esse = would
depart

Total: 70

Exercise 17.2

1 From the passage give an example of:

  (a) an ablative absolute. (1)

  (b) an imperfect subjunctive. (1)

  (c) a present infinitive active. (1)

2 redierant (line 2). Give the person, number and tense of this verb. Give the
1st person singular of the present tense of this verb. (4)

3 multos annos (line 4). In which case is this phrase? Why is this case used? (2)

4 putabant (line 8). Explain the connection between this Latin word and the
English word *reputation*. (1)

Total: 10

→ Indirect statements: accusative and future infinitive

An indirect statement may refer to an action in the future:

> **Example**
>
> scio puellam venturam esse.
> I know that the girl **will** come.
>
> sciebam puellam venturam esse.
> I knew that the girl **would** come.

Exercise 17.3

Translate the following into English:

1 magister scit puerum laboraturum esse.

2 magister scit pueros laboraturos esse.

3 magister sciebat puerum laboraturum esse.

4 magister sciebat pueros laboraturos esse.

5 magister scit puellam laboraturam esse.

6 magister scit puellas laboraturas esse.

7 magister sciebat puellam laboraturam esse.

8 magister sciebat puellas laboraturas esse.

9 scio periculum magnum futurum esse.

10 sciebam pericula magna futura esse.

5 marks for each question. Total: 50

Exercise 17.4

Translate the following into English:

1 magister scit hunc puerum bene laboraturum esse. (7)

2 scio me multum pecuniae numquam habiturum esse. (7)

3 vir credit puellam mox venturam esse. (6)

4 vir credebat puellam mox venturam esse. (6)

5 dux dicit bellum longum futurum esse. (6)

6 dux dixit bellum longum futurum esse. (6)

7 nuntius nuntiavit hostes mox adventuros esse. (6)

8 omnes sciebant Graecos Troiam deleturos esse. (6)

9 sciunt illum servum hoc non facturum esse. (7)

10 servus dixit se brevi tempore dominum interfecturum esse. (8)

Total: 65

Chapter 17

Exercise 17.5

Translate the following into English:

1 scio hunc discipulum numquam laboraturum esse.   (6)

2 spero illam puellam mox venturam esse.   (6)

3 servi sperant se a domino non punitum iri.   (8)

4 nautae sperant hanc tempestatem magnam non fore.   (7)

5 servi sciebant hoc opus difficile futurum esse.   (7)

6 Romani credebant se Graecos mox victuros esse.   (7)

7 non credo te hoc facturum esse.   (6)

8 dux credebat se ante noctem ad urbem adventurum esse.   (9)

9 discipuli sperabant magistrum non adventurum esse.   (6)

10 dominus sciebat illos servos hoc non facturos esse.   (8)

Total: 70

Exercise 17.6

Translate the following into English:

1 Menelaus dixit se magnas copias collecturum esse.   (7)

2 Menelaus dixit se urbem Troiam deleturum esse.   (7)

3 Graeci dixerunt se auxilium ad Menelaum missuros esse.   (8)

4 Menelaus sciebat multos milites multasque naves mox
   adventuros esse.   (9)

5 Menelaus dixit se exercitum contra Troianos missurum esse.   (8)

6 Menelaus dixit exercitum contra Troianos missum iri.   (7)

7 Graeci dixerunt se Troianos punituros esse.   (6)

8 Graeci dixerunt se urbem Troiam mox capturos esse.   (8)

9 Graeci sciebant Troianos urbem fortiter defensuros esse.   (7)

10 Troiani credebant se a Graecis numquam superatum iri.   (8)

Total: 75

Exercise 17.7

Translate the following into English:

1 Graeci sciebant cives Troianos fortiter pugnaturos esse.   (7)

2 Graeci credebant hoc bellum longum futurum esse.   (7)

3 Troiani sciebant se a Graecis tandem victum iri.   (8)

4 Troiani nesciebant Graecos equum ingentem aedificaturos esse.   (7)

5 Troiani dixerunt se equum in urbem ducturos esse.   (8)

6 Aeolus dixit se saccum ventorum Ulixi daturum esse.   (8)

7 Ulixes nesciebat comites suos hoc facturos esse.   (7)

8 Penelope sciebat se coniugem suum diu non visuram esse.   (9)

9 Penelope sperabat Ulixem domum mox rediturum esse.   (7)

10 proci sperabant Penelopen coniugem novum electuram esse.   (7)

Total: 75

Exercise 17.8

Translate the following into Latin:

1 Penelope hopes that Ulixes will return home soon.   (6)

2 I thought that this pupil would work well and for a long time.   (7)

3 We believe that the ships will arrive tomorrow.   (4)

4 You (sing.) know that the soldiers will fight well.   (4)

5 You (sing.) knew that the soldiers would fight well.   (4)

Total: 25

Exercise 17.9

Translate the following into Latin:

1 The general knew that this soldier would be bold.   (6)

2 We hear that the teacher will write a long book.   (5)

3 The citizens knew that the enemy would attack the walls of the city. (6)

4 Ulixes did not know that his companions would do this.   (5)

5 That teacher thinks that all girls will always work well.   (8)

Total: 30

➡ Revision

Exercise 17.10

Give the person, number, tense, mood, voice and the 1st person singular of the present indicative active of the following:

1 eligeret.   6 progressus esset.

2 sperarent.   7 scirent.

3 posses.   8 iisset/ivisset.

4 currerent.   9 persuaderem.

5 cucurrissetis.   10 potuisses.

6 marks for each question. Total: 60

Exercise 17.11

Give and translate the following verb parts:

1 The 1st person singular, imperfect indicative active of puto.

2 The 3rd person plural, perfect indicative active of eligo.

3 The 2nd person singular, future indicative active of spero.

4 The 3rd person plural, pluperfect indicative deponent of progredior.

5 The 1st person plural, imperfect indicative active of scio.

6 The 1st person plural, future indicative deponent of morior.

7 The 3rd person plural, pluperfect indicative active of iuvo.

8 The 3rd person singular, perfect indicative active of impero.

9 The 3rd person singular, pluperfect indicative active of persuadeo.

10 The 2nd person plural, perfect indicative passive of cogo.

2 marks for each question. Total: 20

Exercise 17.12

Translate the following into English:

1 his visis timebam. (3)

2 ubi urbem intravi, multa corpora vidi. (6)

3 celeriter currimus. (2)

4 puer puellam sequebatur quod eam amabat. (6)

5 iuvenis, quod multum vini biberat, ambulare non poterat. (8)

Total: 25

Exercise 18.1

Translate the following passage. Line numbers are given on the left. New words are underlined in the text and their meanings given in the margin.

Athena gives Odysseus some advice

1 Ulixes, ad insulam Ithacam auxilio <u>Phaeacum</u>
latus, <u>tam</u> fessus erat ut in <u>litore</u> dormiret. dea
Athena eum tandem <u>excitavit</u> et ei haec verba
locuta est: '<u>surge</u>, Ulixes! nescio cur dormias.
5 noli prope <u>litus</u> manere! ad regiam progredi
<u>debes</u> ut <u>cognoscas</u> quid ibi <u>agatur</u>. multi proci
adsunt. vinum tuum bibunt. cibum tuum
consumunt. <u>Penelopen</u>, uxorem tuam, <u>in</u>
<u>matrimonium ducere</u> volunt ut tuas <u>divitias</u>
10 <u>comparent</u>. ego te, ut omnia <u>secreto</u>
<u>cognoscas</u>, <u>in mendicum mutabo</u>. sic non
<u>agnosceris</u>. nemo sciet quis <u>re vera</u> sis.' dea,
haec verba locuta, Ulixem in <u>mendicum</u>
<u>mutavit</u>. ille, a <u>litore</u> profectus, ad regiam suam
15 mox advenit.

Phaeaces, -um, m. pl. = the
Phaeacians
tam = so
litus, litoris, n. = beach, shore
excito, -are, -avi, -atum (1) =
I wake (someone) up
surgo, -ere, surrexi,
surrectum (3) = I get up
debeo, -ere, debui, debitum
(2) + *infinitive* = I ought to, must
cognosco, -ere, cognovi,
cognitum (3) = I find out, get
to know
ago, -ere, egi, actum (3) = I do
Penelopen = accusative of
Penelope (Greek form)
in matrimonium duco, -ere,
duxi, ductum (3) = I marry
divitiae, -arum, f. pl. =
wealth, riches
comparo, -are, -avi, -atum
(1) = I gain
secreto = secretly
mendicus, -i, m. = beggar
muto, -are, -avi, -atum (1) =
I change
agnosco, -ere, agnovi,
agnitum (3) = I recognise
re vera = really

Total: 70

Exercise 18.2

1 From the passage give an example of:

  (a) a deponent verb.   (1)

  (b) an imperfect subjunctive.   (1)

  (c) a personal pronoun.   (1)

2 latus (line 2). Give the 1st person singular, present indicative active of
  this verb, and its English meaning.   (2)

3 volunt (line 9). Give the present infinitive active of this verb.   (1)

4 omnia (line 10). In which case is this? Why is this case used?   (2)

5 agnosceris (line 12). Give the tense and voice of this verb.   (2)

Total: 10

→ Present independent subjunctive

The present subjunctive is often used to express an exhortation:

Examples

intret!	**Let** him come in!
hic diu maneamus!	**Let's** stay here for a long time!
bene pugnemus!	**Let's** fight well!
ne hoc faciamus!	**Let's** not do this!

Exercise 18.3

Translate the following into English:

1 intremus!

2 ne rideamus!

3 maneant!

4 eamus!

5 discedamus!

6 navigemus!

7 curramus!

8 dormiam!

9 puniantur!

10 audiar!

2 marks for each question. Total: 20

Exercise 18.4

Translate the following into English:

1 ne interficiatur, miles! (3)

2 bene laboremus, Romani! (3)

3 ne a Romanis superemur! (4)

4 oppidum oppugnemus! (2)

5 vinum nunc bibatur! (3)

6 servi puniantur! (2)

7 rex bene regat! (3)

8 discipuli bene laborent! (3)

9 tela nostra iaciamus! (3)

10 milites a duce laudentur! (4)

Total: 30

Exercise 18.5

Translate the following into English:

1 omnes terrae a Romanis bene regantur! (6)

2 urbem bene defendamus! (3)

3 multum vini bibamus! (3)

4 ne hostes timeamus! (3)

5 celeriter effugiamus! (2)

6 ne a magistro conspiciamur! (4)

7 fortes et audaces simus! (4)

8 magistrum laudemus! (2)

9 equum in urbem ducamus! (4)

10 ne ab hostibus vincamur! (4)

Total: 35

Exercise 18.6

Translate the following into English:

1 discipuli bene laborant ut sapientes sint. (6)

2 curro ut domum celeriter adveniam. (5)

3 principes ad Graeciam redeunt ut coniuges iterum videant. (8)

4 Graeci equum ingentem aedificant ut Troiam capiant. (8)

5 hic servus celeriter currit ne a domino conspiciatur. (8)

6 cives fortiter pugnant ut urbem defendant. (6)

7 cives Troiani bene pugnant ne a Graecis capiantur. (7)

8 celeriter currere volo ut ex periculo effugere possim. (8)

9 hostes veniunt ut nos necent! (5)

10 hic discipulus bene semper laborat ne a magistro puniatur. (9)

Total: 70

Exercise 18.7

Translate the following into English:

1 te moneo ut hoc statim facias. (6)

2 te moneo ne hoc iterum facias. (6)

3 magister pueros semper monet ut laborent. (6)

4 te moneo ne malus sis. (5)

5 filiam monebo ne in via ludat. (6)

6 tibi impero ut labores. (4)

7 puerum moneo ut domum eat. (5)

8 hic magister mihi numquam persuadebit ut laborem. (7)

9 dux sapiens milites semper hortatur ut bene pugnent. (8)

10 dux nautis imperat ut ad Italiam navigent. (7)

Total: 60

Chapter 18

Exercise 18.8

Translate the following into Latin:

1	Let's get up!	(1)
2	Let's hurry!	(1)
3	Let us not be beaten!	(2)
4	Let's advance!	(1)
5	Let him decide today!	(2)
6	Let's cross the river there!	(3)
7	Let them attack the city!	(2)
8	Let's wait for the girls here!	(3)
9	Let's not listen to the teacher!	(3)
10	Let's ask father!	(2)

Total: 20

Exercise 18.9

Translate the following into Latin:

1   The teacher is ordering the girl to work.

2   I will persuade my father to give me the money.

3   We will encourage the soldiers to attack the town.

4   The master orders the slaves not to speak.

5   I advise you not to do this.

5 marks for each question. Total: 25

Exercise 18.10

Translate the following into Latin:

1	I am hurrying to see a girl near the harbour.	(6)
2	We are fighting to defend our city.	(5)
3	He is going to the harbour to wait for a ship.	(6)
4	The ship is departing in order to sail to the island.	(6)
5	The soldiers are collecting their weapons in order to fight against the enemy.	(7)

Total: 30

Exercise 18.11

Translate the following into English:

1	quid nunc facere debeo?	(4)
2	domum festinare debes.	(3)
3	hoc mox facere debes.	(4)

4 statim surgere debes, puer! (4)

5 hunc librum legere debeo. (4)

6 puellae parvae numquam flere debent. (5)

7 bene pugnare debebimus, milites! (4)

8 discipuli boni magistros audire debent. (5)

9 magistrum audire debetis, pueri! (4)

10 pueri parvi in media via stare non debent. (8)

Total: 45

Exercise 18.12

Translate the following into English:

1 milites boni bene pugnare debent. (5)

2 multa praemia accipere debemus. (4)

3 naves mox proficisci debent. (4)

4 iuvenes vinum bibere non debent. (5)

5 milites gladios et scuta semper ferre debent. (7)

6 magistri discipulos bonos laudare semper debent. (6)

7 discipuli boni a magistris laudari semper debent. (7)

8 servus tuus bene laborare debet. (5)

9 fortes in hoc proelio esse debebimus, comites! (7)

10 ex urbe discedere nunc debeo. (5)

Total: 55

Exercise 18.13

Translate the following into Latin:

1 I must hurry. (2)

2 The messenger ought to run. (3)

3 You (sing.) ought to work. (2)

4 Kings have to rule. (3)

5 You (pl.) should not shout. (2)

6 The citizens will have to work well. (4)

7 We have to capture this city. (4)

8 I must leave immediately. (3)

9 What must we do? (3)

10 Now we ought to write a book. (4)

Total: 30

→ Revision

Exercise 18.14

Give the person, number, tense, mood, voice and the 1st person singular of the present indicative active of the following:

1 sit.

2 esset.

3 fuisset.

4 essent.

5 viderentur.

6 irent.

7 surrexisses.

8 vincamur.

9 velimus.

10 cognovisset.

6 marks for each question. Total: 60

Exercise 18.15

Translate the following into English:

1 ille rex ab omnibus civibus non amabatur.   (7)

2 non omnes cives regem amabant.   (5)

3 dux milites ad flumen statim progredi iussit.   (7)

4 ille senex sapiens est. multa scit.   (6)

5 omnes in urbem cras ibimus.   (5)

Total: 30

19

Exercise 19.1

Translate the following passage. Line numbers are given on the left. New words are underlined in the text and their meanings given in the margin.

Telemachus scolds the suitors, but they are too drunk to pay attention

1 Penelope, uxor Ulixis, Telemachusque, filius
Ulixis, in regia erant. proci quoque ibi aderant:
vinum bibebant cibumque consumebant. multi
eorum <u>tantum</u> vini biberant <u>ut</u> <u>ebrii</u> essent.

5 Telemachus, procis <u>ebriis</u> visis, <u>tam</u> iratus erat <u>ut</u>
eos <u>reprehendere</u> constituerit. ad eos progressus
haec verba dixit: 'nobiles, semper hic adestis;
semper cibum nostrum consumitis. nunc <u>tantum</u>
vini bibistis <u>ut</u> <u>ebrii</u> sitis. ego scio cur hic adsitis.

10 mater tamen mea non credit Ulixem mortuum
esse. scit illum mox hic adfuturum esse. cur in
regia nostra manetis? pessimi estis! <u>hinc</u>
discedite!' proci tamen Telemacho non
responderunt. <u>tam</u> <u>ebrii</u> erant <u>ut</u> non audirent

15 quid filius Ulixis diceret.

tantum = so much
ut = that
ebrius, -a, -um = drunk
tam = so
reprehendo, -ere,
reprehendi, reprehensum
(3) = I tell off

hinc = from here

Total: 90

Exercise 19.2

1 From the passage give an example of:

(a) a noun in the ablative. (1)

(b) an imperfect subjunctive. (1)

(c) a deponent verb. (1)

2 biberant (line 4). Give the person, number and tense of this verb. (3)

3 eos (line 6). Give the nominative masculine singular of this pronoun. (1)

4 mortuum (line 10). Explain the connection between this Latin word and the English word *mortuary*. (1)

5 pessimi (line 12). This is a superlative adjective. Give the positive and comparative forms of this adjective in the nominative masculine singular. (2)

Total: 10

→ Consecutive clauses

These indicate consequences – something which happens as a result of something else. In English the fact that a consecutive clause is coming up is given away by **early warning words** like **so** or **such**. The consecutive clause itself is introduced by the word **that**, meaning 'with the result that …'

Examples

He is **so** stupid **that** he doesn't know any Latin.

She was **such** a good runner **that** she won lots of prizes.

He drank **so much** beer **that** he soon became drunk.

English: Early warning word so/such + adjective/adverb/verb + that (= with the result that …)

Latin	English
tam	so
adeo	so, to such an extent
tantus	so great
tot	so many (not tam multi!)
totiens	so often, so many times
talis	such, of such a kind
ita	in such a way

Examples

1 tam fessus est ut currere non possit.

   He is so tired that he cannot run (present).

2 tot vulnerati sunt ut Romani victi sint.

   So many were wounded that the Romans were beaten (perfect).

3 puer adeo timebat ut dormire non posset.

   The boy was so scared that he was not able to sleep (imperfect).

(Exercise 19.3)

Translate the following into English:

1 tam superbus sum ut nemo me amet.   (7)

2 puer tam malus erat ut nemo eum amaret.   (8)

3 tot tela ab hostibus iacta sunt ut multi vulnerati sint.   (10)

4 milites iter tam longum fecerant ut fessi essent.   (8)

5 hoc vinum tam bonum est ut id saepe bibam.   (9)

6 magister tam crudelis erat ut ab omnibus timeretur.   (8)

7 puer tam fessus erat ut bene dormiverit.   (7)

8 nuntius tam celeriter cucurrit ut ad urbem ante noctem advenerit. (10)

9 proelium tam saevum erat ut multi milites mortui sint.   (9)

10 magister tam bonus erat ut ab omnibus discipulis amaretur.   (9)

Total: 85

Exercise 19.4

Translate the following into English:

1 illa femina tam tristis erat ut fleret. (7)

2 milites adeo timebant ut fugerint. (5)

3 tam bene laboro ut a magistro saepe lauder. (8)

4 ille dominus tam crudelis est ut omnes servi eum timeant. (10)

5 ille dominus tam crudelis erat ut omnes servi eum timerent. (10)

6 Graeci adeo timebant ut ad naves celeriter cucurrerint. (8)

7 Graeci in tanto periculo erant ut effugere constituerint. (8)

8 hic puer tam bonus est ut magister eum saepe laudet. (10)

9 illa puella tam pulchra erat ut omnes eam amarent. (9)

10 ille servus tam bene laborabat ut dominus pecuniam ei dederit. (10)

Total: 85

Exercise 19.5

Translate the following into English:

1 Romani tam bene pugnaverunt ut hostes urbem capere non possent. (10)

2 naves tam celeres erant ut Graeci effugere possent. (8)

3 tempestas tam saeva erat ut omnes naves deleverit. (8)

4 tempestas tam saeva erat ut omnes naves deletae sint. (9)

5 Romani tam audaces erant ut oppidum mox ceperint. (8)

6 hoc opus tam difficile est ut id facere non possim. (10)

7 Romani tam fortes erant ut hostes celeriter superaverint. (8)

8 tot hostes erant ut timeremus. (5)

9 tot homines in via erant ut currere non possemus. (9)

10 Romani muros ita aedificaverant ut hostes eos delere non possent. (10)

Total: 85

Exercise 19.6

Translate the following into English:

1 ille miles tot vulnera accepit ut tandem ambulare non posset. (10)

2 servus dominum saevum adeo timebat ut effugere constituerit. (8)

3 tot hostes erant ut victi simus. (6)

4 adeo vulneratus erat ut currere non posset. (7)

5 discipuli tam fessi sunt ut semper dormiant. (7)

6 ille senex totiens loquitur ut nemo eum audiat. (8)

7 illa femina tam pulchra est ut a multis viris ametur. (10)

8 venti tam fortes erant ut navem ad insulam celeriter pepulerint. (10)

9 venti tam fortes erant ut navis ad insulam celeriter pulsa sit. (11)

10 tantum scutum habebat ut nullum vulnus passus sit. (8)

Total: 85

→ Revision

Exercise 19.7

Translate and name the major construction featured in each of the following sentences:

1 tot hostes erant ut Romani timerent. (6 + 1)

2 audivi multos milites interfectos esse. (5 + 1)

3 te moneo ne hoc facias. (5 + 1)

4 puer dixit se illam puellam amare. (6 + 1)

5 pueri libros legere debent ut sapientes sint. (7 + 1)

6 tot sagittae iactae sunt ut caelum videre non possemus. (9 + 1)

7 pater filios hortatus est ne vinum biberent. (7 + 1)

8 rex dixit Romanos exercitum magnum paravisse. (6 + 1)

9 rex tamen militibus imperavit ut servos liberarent. (7 + 1)

10 amicus meus putat urbem mox captum iri. (7 + 1)

Total: 75

Exercise 19.8

Give the person, number, tense, voice and the 1st person singular of the present indicative active of the following subjunctives:

1 ageretur.

2 cognoscamus.

3 audirent.

4 fecerim.

5 mortuus sit.

6 fuerit.

7 deberemus.

8 coactus esset.

9 actus sis.

10 capiamur.

5 marks for each question. Total: 50

Exercise 19.9

Translate the following into Latin:

1 I work so well that my teacher is always praising me.   (9)

2 So many people were in the city that we were not able to see the queen. (9)

3 He fights so often that he is never afraid of danger.   (8)

4 The girl was so tired that she wanted to sleep.   (7)

5 The danger was so great that day that we were afraid.   (7)

Total: 40

Exercise 19.10

Translate the following into Latin:

1 This book is so long that I cannot read it.   (9)

2 That teacher was so cruel that everyone was afraid of him.   (9)

3 That task was so difficult that no one was able to do it.   (10)

4 The queen was so beautiful that she was loved by everyone.   (8)

5 I speak so often in the town that no one listens to me.   (9)

Total: 45

Exercise 19.11

Translate the following into English:

1 multi cives ad oppidum hodie eunt.   (6)

2 his verbis dictis tandem discessimus.   (5)

3 dux magna voce clamavit.   (4)

4 vulnus ab illo milite acceptum erat.   (6)

5 hostes oppidum captum deleverunt.   (4)

Total: 25

Exercise 20.1

Translate the following passage. Line numbers are given on the left. New words are underlined in the text and their meanings given in the margin.

Penelope questions the beggar

1 dum Telemachus haec verba procis loquitur,
Penelope mendicum <u>veterem</u> prope <u>limen</u>
stantem <u>animadvertit</u>. nesciebat hunc mendicum
suum coniugem esse. ei persuasit ut intraret.

5 deinde, cum procis imperavisset ut cibum
mendico darent, eum rogavit quis esset, <u>unde</u>
venisset, quid vellet, <u>quo</u> iret. mendicus respondit
se <u>divitem</u> olim fuisse sed, multa mala passum,
nunc <u>pauperem</u> esse. dixit se in regia paucos

10 dies manere et cibum a procis petere velle.
Penelope, verbis mendici auditis, 'nobiscum
mane, mendice,' inquit. 'ego filio meo ut te <u>curet</u>,
procis ut cibum tibi dent, imperabo.' haec verba
locuta ad <u>cubiculum</u> suum discessit.

vetus, veteris = old
limen, liminis, n. = doorway
animadverto, -ere, -verti,
-versum (3) = I notice

unde = where ... from
quo = where ... to
dives, divitis = rich
pauper, pauperis = poor

curo, -are, -avi, -atum (1) =
I look after, I care for
cubiculum, -i, n. = bedroom

Total: 90

Exercise 20.2

1 From the passage give an example of:

(a) a pluperfect subjunctive. (1)

(b) a perfect infinitive. (1)

(c) a reflexive pronoun. (1)

(d) a present subjunctive. (1)

2 loquitur (line 1). What name is given to this sort of verb? (1)

3 stantem (line 3). What part of the verb sto is this? (1)

4 imperavisset (line 5). Explain the connection between this Latin word
and the English word *imperial*. (1)

5 darent (line 6). In which mood is this verb? Why is this mood used? (2)

6 velle (line 10). Give the 1st person singular, present indicative active
of this verb. (1)

Total: 10

→ Indirect questions

The verb in an indirect question goes into the subjunctive. It uses the same tense as the English.

> **Examples**
> 1 scio quid **faciat**.
>   I know what he is doing. (present subjunctive)
> 2 scio quid **fecerit**.
>   I know what he has done. (perfect subjunctive)
> 3 rogavi cur **venisset**.
>   I asked why he had come. (pluperfect subjunctive)
> 4 rogavi quid **vellet**.
>   I asked what he wanted. (imperfect subjunctive)

Special vocabulary

num	whether
utrum … an	whether … or
utrum … necne	whether … or not

Note on the future

Where the indirect question refers to the future, we use the future participle plus the subjunctive of **sum**:

> **Examples**
> scio quid factura sit. (present subjunctive of sum)
> I know what she will do. (= is about to do)
> sciebam quid factura esset. (imperfect subjunctive of sum)
> I knew what she would do. (= was about to do)

Exercise 20.3

Translate the following into English:

1 nescio quis sis. (3)

2 scio ubi habitet. (3)

3 sciebam ubi habitaret. (3)

4 puerum captum rogavi quid faceret. (5)

5 pueros captos rogavi quid facerent. (5)

6 nescio cur festines. (3)

7 nescio cur hoc feceris. (4)

8 eum rogavi ubi habitaret. (4)

9 ille magister nescit quid faciat. (5)

10 ille magister nesciebat quid faceret. (5)

Total: 40

Exercise 20.4

Translate the following into English:

1 pater filium rogat cur vinum bibat.   (6)

2 pater filium rogat cur vinum biberit.   (6)

3 pater filium rogavit quid biberet.   (5)

4 pater filium rogavit quid bibisset.   (5)

5 nescio quid fecerit.   (3)

6 nescio quis veniat.   (3)

7 nescio quis venerit.   (3)

8 nesciebam quis veniret.   (3)

9 nesciebam quis venisset.   (3)

10 sciebamus cur festinarent.   (3)

Total: 40

Exercise 20.5

Translate the following into English:

1 quis vestrum scit ubi hic puer habitet?   (7)

2 puerum rogavi quid hic faceret.   (5)

3 puerum rogavi quid fecisset.   (4)

4 nescio cur hic puer tam fessus sit.   (7)

5 nuntius nuntiavit ubi hostes essent.   (5)

6 mater nesciebat ubi filia esset.   (5)

7 magister discipulos rogavit cur riderent.   (5)

8 magister discipulos rogat cur non laborent.   (6)

9 magister discipulos rogavit cur non laborarent.   (6)

10 puer puellam rogavit cur fleret.   (5)

Total: 55

Exercise 20.6

Translate the following into English:

1 vir dominum rogavit cur servum punivisset.   (6)

2 Romani nesciebant cur urbs ab hostibus oppugnaretur.   (7)

3 Romani nesciebant cur hostes urbem oppugnavissent.   (6)

4 agricola servum rogavit num equos in agris vidisset.   (8)

5 dux cognoscere volebat ubi hostes essent.   (6)

6 dux milites rogavit cur venissent et quid vellent. (8)

7 magister nesciebat utrum puella rideret necne. (6)

8 nescio utrum hi pueri laborent an ludant. (7)

9 nescimus cur servus haec verba dixerit. (6)

10 tandem cognovimus quid hostes facerent. (5)

Total: 65

Exercise 20.7

Translate the following into English:

1 Troiani nesciebant cur Graeci equum ingentem in litore posuissent. (9)

2 Troiani nesciebant cur equus ingens in litore a Graecis positus esset. (11)

3 Troiani nesciebant cur equus ingens in litore staret. (8)

4 Troiani nesciebant cur Graeci tum discessissent. (6)

5 Troiani nesciebant num milites Graeci in equo essent. (8)

6 Troiani nesciebant utrum equum delere an accipere deberent. (8)

7 Troiani nesciebant utrum equum in urbem ducere deberent necne. (9)

8 Troiani nesciebant quid facere deberent. (5)

9 Graeci nesciebant quid Troiani facturi essent. (6)

10 Graeci nesciebant utrum Troiani equum in urbem ducturi essent necne. (10)

Total: 80

Exercise 20.8

Translate the following into English:

1 nemo sciebat quis mendicus esset. (5)

2 Penelope mendicum rogavit unde venisset. (5)

3 Penelope eum rogavit cur in regia esset. (7)

4 Penelope eum rogavit quid vellet. (5)

5 Penelope eum rogavit quo iret. (5)

6 Penelope eum rogavit cur pauper esset. (6)

7 Penelope eum rogavit utrum laetus esset necne. (7)

8 Telemachus procos rogavit cur vinum semper biberent. (7)

9 mendicus cognoscere volebat utrum Telemachus fortis esset necne. (8)

10 Telemachus nesciebat quid facere deberet. (5)

Total: 60

→ Revision

Exercise 20.9

Translate and name the major construction featured in each of the following sentences:

1 scio ubi Marcus habitet. (4 + 1)

2 nescio quis sis. (3 + 1)

3 nuntius dixit se librum ferre. (5 + 1)

4 magister tam stultus erat ut nemo eum audiret. (8 + 1)

5 puella adeo timebat ut fleret. (5 + 1)

6 ad urbem ibo ut reginam videam. (5 + 1)

7 Romani audiverunt hostes appropinquare. (4 + 1)

8 dixit se mox venturum esse. (5 + 1)

9 celeriter curro ne a magistro capiar. (6 + 1)

10 audio hunc puerum stultissimum esse. (5 + 1)

stultus = stupid

Total: 60

Exercise 20.10

Give the person, number, tense, voice and the 1st person singular of the present indicative active of the following subjunctives:

1 animadvertissem.   6 latus sim.

2 mutemus.   7 curarent.

3 ferrentur.   8 sequeretur.

4 nollemus.   9 pellamur.

5 credamus.   10 interficerentur.

5 marks for each question. Total: 50

Exercise 20.11

Translate the following into Latin:

1 I know who you are.

2 We know where you live.

3 I do not know why you are crying.

4 He knows where we are going (to).

5 They know where you have come from.

3 marks for each question. Total: 15

Chapter 20

126

Exercise 20.12

Translate the following into Latin:

1 After the battle the soldiers did not know what they ought to do. (6)

2 The general asked the soldiers why they were not fighting. (6)

3 The general asked the soldiers why they had not attacked the city. (7)

4 The general asked the soldiers whether they were scared. (5)

5 I asked the girl whether she was laughing or crying. (6)

Total: 30

Exercise 20.13

Translate the following into English:

1 dux milites audaces et fortes esse iussit. (7)

2 nautae audaciores naves celeriores amant. (5)

3 ubi habitat Marcus? nescimus. (4)

4 equi ex agro ab agricola acti sunt. (7)

5 multae villae in illo bello deletae sunt. (7)

Total: 30

Exercise 21.1

Translate the following passage. Line numbers are given on the left. New words are underlined in the text and their meanings given in the margin.

Odysseus decides to kill the suitors. Penelope decides to choose a new husband

1 Ulixes, ubi superbiam procorum vidit, tam iratus
  factus est ut omnes procos occidere constituerit.
  veritus tamen ne hoc solus facere non posset,
  deam Athenam auxilium rogare et Telemacho
5 dicere se re vera patrem Ulixem esse constituit.

  Penelope interea, quae coniugem novum eligere
  constituerat, procis convocatis haec verba locuta
  est: 'multos annos Ulixes meus abest. timeo ne
  illum numquam iterum videam. is igitur qui arcum
10 Ulixis capere et sagittam per duodecim secures
  mittere poterit, coniunx meus erit.' proci, his
  verbis auditis, inter se spectabant. solliciti erant.
  timebant ne hoc facere non possent. Antinous
  autem putavit se optimum procorum esse;
15 credebat se hoc facere posse.

superbia, -ae, f. = arrogance
fio, fieri, factus sum = I become, I am made
veritus = fearing
ne = that

eligo, -ere, elegi, electum (3) = I choose
convoco, -are, -avi, -atum (1) = I call together
arcus, -us, m. = bow
securis, -is, f. = axe

sollicitus, -a -um = worried
puto, -are, -avi, -atum (1) = I think

Total: 90

Exercise 21.2

1 From the passage give an example of:

   (a) a perfect subjunctive. (1)

   (b) a deponent verb. (1)

   (c) a relative pronoun. (1)

2 multos annos (line 8). In which case is this expression? Why is this
   case used? (2)

3 abest (line 8). Give the person, number, tense and 1st person singular of
   the present indicative active of this verb. (4)

4 optimum (line 14). This is a superlative adjective. Give the nominative
   masculine singular of its positive form. (1)

Total: 10

→ Fear clauses

Fearing, being afraid **to do** something
timeo + **infinitive'**

> **Example**
>
> milites **pugnare** timebant.
> The soldiers were afraid **to fight.**

Fearing, being afraid **that** ...
timeo, vereor + ne + **verb in subjunctive**

> **Examples**
>
> timeo ne **veniat.**
> I am afraid that he **will, may come.**
>
> timebam ne **veniret.**
> I was afraid that he **would, might come.**
>
> timeo ne **veniat.**
> I am afraid that he **is coming.**
>
> timebam ne **veniret.**
> I was afraid that he **was coming.**
>
> timeo ne **venerit.**
> I am afraid that **he came.**
>
> timebam ne **venisset.**
> I was afraid that he **had come.**

Exercise 21.3

Translate the following into English:

1 timeo ne hoc facere non possim.   (6)

2 nuntius timebat ne dux sibi non crederet.   (7)

3 veritus ne cives diu pugnarent, dux oppidum statim
   oppugnare constituit.   (10)

4 veriti ne a domino punirentur, servi effugerunt.   (7)

5 omnes discipuli timent ne magister mox adveniat.   (7)

6 miles, veritus ne amicus interficeretur, fortiter pugnavit.   (7)

7 verebamur ne omnes naves deletae essent.   (6)

8 timebam ne frater meus a patre puniretur.   (7)

9 dominus veretur ne servi effugere conentur.   (6)

10 cives timebant ne hostes urbem mox oppugnarent.   (7)

Total: 70

Exercise 21.4

Translate the following into English:

1 servi timebant ne a domino occiderentur. (6)

2 mater verebatur ne filius in illo proelio mortuus esset. (9)

3 dominus magnopere timebat ne servum necavisset. (6)

4 puer timet ne hoc opus non fecerit. (7)

5 milites verebantur ne ab hostibus caperentur. (6)

6 nauta timebat ne navis tempestate deleretur. (6)

7 nauta timebat ne tempestas navem deleret. (6)

8 discipuli timebant ne a magistro punirentur. (6)

9 veritae ne viri in bello perirent, uxores eos rogaverunt ne irent. (11)

10 timeo ne hostes magnas copias hodie parent. (7)

Total: 70

Exercise 21.5

Translate the following into English:

1 Menelaus timebat ne Helena ad urbem Troiam a Paride ducta esset. (11)

2 Graeci timebant ne Troiam celeriter non caperent. (7)

3 Graeci, veriti ne Troia numquam caperetur, equum ingentem fecerunt. (9)

4 Ulixes verebatur ne domum numquam rediret. (6)

5 verita ne vir non rediret, Penelope saepe flebat. (8)

6 Graeci timebant ne a Polyphemo interficerentur. (6)

7 Ulixes timebat ne ipse omnes procos solus occidere non posset. (10)

8 Penelope timebat ne virum numquam iterum videret. (7)

9 Penelope timebat ne vir in bello occisus esset. (8)

10 cives Troiani timebant ne urbs a Graecis caperetur. (8)

Total: 80

Exercise 21.6

Translate the following into Latin:

1 I am greatly afraid that we may be killed. (4)

2 I was afraid that that old man would do this. (6)

3 The boy was afraid that his mother would be worried. (7)

4 All the sailors were afraid that storms would destroy the ship. (7)

5 The slave was afraid that his master had heard him shouting. (6)

Total: 30

Exercise 21.7

Translate the following into Latin:

1 Fearing that I would be punished, I fled. (4)

2 Fearing that the teacher would be angry, the pupils said nothing. (6)

3 Fearing that her mother had seen her, the girl ran. (7)

4 Fearing that the city would be taken, the soldiers fought bravely. (7)

5 Fearing that their husbands had been killed, the women were crying. (6)

Total: 30

→ Revision

Exercise 21.8

Translate and name the major construction featured in each of the following sentences:

1 dux cognovit quid hostes pararent. (5 + 1)

2 dux cognovit quid ab hostibus pararetur. (6 + 1)

3 castra* nostra tanta sunt ut hostes ea capere non possint. (10 + 1)

4 milites sciebant se ab hostibus victum iri. (7 + 1)

5 hostes currebant ne a Romanis interficerentur. (6 + 1)

6 nescio cur mulieres festinent. (4 + 1)

7 nautae urbem intraverunt ut cibum emerent. (6 + 1)

8 amicum rogavi cur nautae urbem intravissent. (6 + 1)

9 amicus respondit nautas cibum emere* velle. (6 + 1)

10 eum rogavi quid faceret. (4 + 1)

*castra, -orum, n. pl. = camp
emo, -ere, emi, emptum (3) = I buy

Total: 70

Exercise 21.9

Translate the following into Latin:

1 hostes celeriter progressi sunt ut Romanos oppugnarent. (7)

2 puer adeo se laudabat ut nemo eum amaret. (8)

3 vir amico dixit se pecuniam ei daturum esse. (7)

4 dux dixit milites suos fortissimos esse. (6)

5 numquam mihi persuadebis ut hoc faciam. (6)

6 ad urbem festinavit ut amicum iuvaret. (6)

7 nesciebamus ubi essemus. (3)

8 dominus servis imperavit ut pecuniam traderent. (6)

9 milites viderunt hostes urbem bene defendere. (6)

10 poetam rogavimus cur haec verba scripsisset. (5)

Total: 60

Exercise 21.10

Give the person, number, tense, voice and the 1st person singular of the present indicative active of the following subjunctives:

1 possimus.

2 esset.

3 servaverint.

4 convocavisset.

5 effugeremus.

6 relinqueret.

7 fiat.

8 reducerentur.

9 ivisset.

10 victi simus.

5 marks for each question. Total: 50

Exercise 21.11

Translate the following into English:

1 noli timere, amice – ego te iuvabo. (6)

2 dominus e villa egressus est. servi eius celeriter secuti sunt. (10)

3 timebamus quod magna turba agricolarum appropinquabat. (6)

4 milites huius regis fortissimi erant. (5)

5 multa verba sapientia ab illo magistro saepe dicuntur. (8)

Total: 35

Exercise 22.1

Translate the following passage. Line numbers are given on the left. New words are underlined in the text and their meanings given in the margin.

The beggar succeeds where the suitors fail

1 Telemachus, ubi mendicus ei dixit se re vera
Ulixem esse, tam laetus erat ut flere <u>inceperit</u>.
Ulixes tamen ei imperavit ut arma procorum
collecta <u>celaret</u>.

incipio, -ere, incepi,
inceptum (3½) = I begin
celo, -are, -avi, -atum (1)
= I hide

5 in media regia interea duodecim <u>secures</u> et <u>arcus</u>
vetus Ulixis a servis <u>Penelopes</u> parati erant. proci
<u>arcum</u> et <u>secures</u> solliciti iam spectabant.
timebant ne <u>arcum</u> <u>intendere</u> non possent.
Antinous <u>arcum</u> primus cepit, nec tamen eum
10 <u>intendere</u> potuit. tum mendicus rogavit ut sibi
<u>arcus</u> traderetur. proci riserunt, veriti ne ille
<u>arcum</u> <u>intendere</u> posset, sed tandem, a
Telemacho iussi, <u>arcum</u> mendico tradiderunt. ille
<u>arcum</u> sine <u>difficultate</u> <u>intendit</u> et sagittam misit.
15 sagitta per omnes secures <u>volavit</u>. <u>silentium</u> fuit.

securis, -is, f. = axe
arcus, -us, m. = bow
Penelopes = genitive of
Penelope (Greek form)
intendo, -ere, intendi,
intentum (3) = I bend
difficultas, difficultatis, f.
= difficulty
volo, -are, -avi, -atum (1)
= I fly

silentium, -i, n. = silence

Total: 80

Exercise 22.2

1 From the passage give an example of:

  (a) a perfect subjunctive. (1)

  (b) a past participle passive. (1)

  (c) a reflexive pronoun. (1)

2 celaret (line 4). In which mood is this verb? Why is this mood used? (2)

3 mendico (line 13). In which case is this noun? (1)

4 tradiderunt (line 13). Give the person, number, tense and 1st person
singular of the present indicative active of this verb. (4)

Total: 10

Exercises 22.3–22.5

Give the person, number, tense, voice and the 1st person singular, present indicative active of each of the following subjunctives:

Exercise 22.3

1 amentur.

2 regant.

3 nolimus.

4 veniret.

5 vidisset.

6 audirentur.

7 moniti essent.

8 sit.

9 cucurrerit.

10 deletus sit.

5 marks for each question. Total: 50

Exercise 22.4

1 putaret.

2 essemus.

3 cognoverit.

4 eamus.

5 curetur.

6 transiret.

7 convocavisset.

8 debeam.

9 surrexissem.

10 scripseris.

5 marks for each question. Total: 50

Exercise 22.5

1 discederetis.

2 occisus sit.

3 caperemur.

4 fuerim.

5 misisses.

6 nollet.

7 pellamur.

8 mansissem.

9 dormiant.

10 irent.

5 marks for each question. Total: 50

Exercise 22.6

Give the 3rd person singular, imperfect subjunctive active of the following verbs:

1 sum.

2 audio.

3 conspicio.

4 duco.

5 eo.

6 occido.

7 ambulo.

8 volo, velle.

9 video.

10 curro.

1 mark for each question. Total: 10

Exercise 22.7

Give the 3rd person plural, imperfect subjunctive passive of the following verbs:

1 vinco.
2 capio.
3 vulnero.
4 punio.
5 audio.

6 occido.
7 oppugno.
8 libero.
9 interficio.
10 video.

1 mark for each question. Total: 10

➜ Revision

Translate and name the major construction featured in each of the following sentences:

Exercise 22.8

1 milites cognoverunt ubi copiae hostium essent. (6 + 1)
2 tot Romani vulnerati sunt ut a Graecis victi sint. (9 + 1)
3 Graeci credebant se Romanos victuros esse. (6 + 1)
4 puerum rogavi utrum rideret an fleret. (6 + 1)
5 dux militibus imperavit ne timerent. (5 + 1)
6 hic murus tam altus est ut eum delere non possimus. (10 + 1)
7 dux milites rogavit num hostes vidissent. (6 + 1)
8 dixit se reginam hostium vidisse. (5 + 1)
9 omnes sciebamus quid Romani vellent. (5 + 1)
10 Troiani timebant ne Troia a Graecis caperetur. (7 + 1)

Total: 75

Exercise 22.9

1 magister pueros rogavit cur non laborarent. (6 + 1)
2 audio hunc magistrum pessimum esse. (5 + 1)
3 mater filiam rogavit quid faceret. (5 + 1)
4 milites tam laeti erant ut magnis vocibus clamarent. (8 + 1)
5 miles hostes adeo timebat ut pugnare nollet. (7 + 1)
6 miles clamavit se pugnare nolle. (5 + 1)
7 miles timebat ne ab hostibus occideretur. (6 + 1)
8 dux militi imperavit ut pugnaret. (6 + 1)
9 miles respondit se numquam pugnaturum esse. (6 + 1)
10 dux militem rogavit cur hoc dixisset. (6 + 1)

Total: 70

Chapter 22

Exercise 22.10

Double-deckers: translate the following and name the **two** major constructions featured in each sentence.

1 dux dixit se venisse ut milites hortaretur. (7 + 2)

2 dux milites hortatus est ut fortes essent ne ab hostibus vincerentur. (11 + 2)

3 nuntii ad urbem venerunt ut cognoscerent quid hostes pararent. (9 + 2)

4 magister tam attonitus* erat ut discipulum rogaverit cur hoc fecisset. (10 + 2)

5 discipulus timebat ne magister rogaret cur hoc fecisset. (8 + 2)

*attonitus = amazed

Total: 55

Exercises 22.11–22.15

Give the tense and the 1st person singular, present indicative active of the following subjunctives:

Exercise 22.11

1 velit.

2 vellet.

3 possemus.

4 essent.

5 fuisset.

6 iret.

7 nollent.

8 videretur.

9 amaverit.

10 deletus sit.

2 marks for each question. Total: 20

Exercise 22.12

1 inceperit.

2 animadvertisset.

3 deberent.

4 sperent.

5 nesciremus.

6 vereretur.

7 cognoscat.

8 putaret.

9 progressus sit.

10 iuvemur.

2 marks for each question. Total: 20

Exercise 22.13

1 ament.

2 rexisset.

3 ceperit.

4 visus esset.

5 dixissent.

6 monerem.

7 audiremus.

8 esset.

9 miserit.

10 curreret.

2 marks for each question. Total: 20

Exercise 22.14

1 persuaserit.

2 coactus esset.

3 ferrent.

4 pellatur.

5 interficeret.

6 tulerit.

7 custodiatur.

8 contenderemus.

9 peterent.

10 crediderit.

2 marks for each question. Total: 20

Exercise 22.15

1 convenissent.

2 reliquerim.

3 occupavisses.

4 vulneraretur.

5 occidisset.

6 effugeret.

7 inveniamus.

8 victi simus.

9 defendamus.

10 conspexissent.

2 marks for each question. Total: 20

Exercise 22.16

Translate the following into English:

1 is est puer, ea est puella, illi sunt dei. (9)

2 Romani contra Graecos gladiis et hastis saepe pugnabant. (8)

3 dominus servum punivit quod malus erat. (6)

4 domus mea maior est quam tua. (6)

5 aqua illius fluminis non clara est. (6)

Total: 35

Exercise 23.1

Translate the following passage. Line numbers are given on the left. New words are underlined in the text and their meanings given in the margin.

The suitors are slaughtered

1 proci mendicum <u>attoniti</u> spectabant. 'Ulixes sum,' clamavit ille. 'domum tandem redii. nunc ego vos omnes puniam. mox omnes mortui eritis.'

haec locutus sagittam ad Antinoum misit.
5 Antinous ad terram <u>cecidit</u> mortuus. <u>tumultus</u> in regia erat. proci, Antinoo mortuo viso, timebant ne ipsi quoque ab Ulixe mox occiderentur. <u>passim discurrebant</u>, arma petentes. <u>nulla</u> erant. Ulixes et Telemachus interea sagittas in eos
10 mittebant. illi adeo timebant ut e regia effugere conati sint. frustra. <u>nulla fuga</u> erat. <u>sanguis passim fluebat</u>. mox per totam regiam <u>iacebant acervi</u> corporum. omnes occisi erant.

attonitus, -a, -um = amazed

cado, -ere, cecidi, casum (3) = I fall, I drop
tumultus, -us, m. = uproar
passim = everywhere
discurro, -ere, discurri, discursum (3) = I run about
nullus, -a, -um = none, no
fuga, -ae, f. = escape
sanguis, sanguinis, m. = blood
fluo, -ere, fluxi, fluxum (3) = I flow
iaceo, -ere, iacui (2) = I lie
acervus, -i, m. = heap, pile

Total: 75

Exercise 23.2

1 From the passage give an example of:

(a) a present participle. (1)

(b) a perfect subjunctive. (1)

2 occiderentur (line 7). In which mood is this verb? (1)

3 arma (line 8). In which case is this noun? (1)

4 occisi erant (line 13). Give the person, number, tense, mood, voice and 1st person singular of the present indicative active of this verb. (6)

Total: 10

→ # Why subjunctive?

Remember, there are seven reasons why a verb may be in the subjunctive.

Reason	Example
1 present independent subjunctive	**eamus!** Let's go!
2 purpose clause	venit **ut luderet**. He came to (in order to) play.
3 indirect command	eum **rogavi ut veniret**. I asked him to come.
4 indirect question	scio **quis sit**. I know who he is.
5 consecutive clause	**tam** fessa est **ut fleat**. She is so tired that she is crying.
6 fear clause	**timebam** ne magister mox **adveniret**. I was afraid that the master would arrive soon.
7 cum-clause (since,when)	**cum** fessus **sit**, ambulare non potest. Since he is tired, he cannot walk.

Exercises 23.3–23.6

Translate the following sentences and state why the underlined verb is in the subjunctive mood.

Exercise 23.3

1 celeriter cucurri ut <u>effugerem</u>. (4 + 1)

2 te rogo ut <u>maneas</u>. (4 + 1)

3 tam saevus est ut nemo eum <u>amet</u>. (7 + 1)

4 puer, cum per viam <u>ambularet</u>, puellam pulchram conspexit. (8 + 1)

5 magister pueros rogavit ne in via <u>luderent</u>. (7 + 1)

6 cum milites <u>progressi essent</u>, contra hostes pugnaverunt. (7 + 1)

7 ad urbem imus ut <u>laboremus</u>. (5 + 1)

8 hostes <u>vincamus</u>, milites! (3 + 1)

9 timeo ne pater meus me <u>puniat</u>. (6 + 1)

10 nesciebam cur puellae <u>currerent</u>. (4 + 1)

Total: 65

Exercise 23.4

1 magister discipulis imperavit ut <u>laborarent</u>. (5 + 1)

2 hic diu <u>maneamus</u> et vinum <u>bibamus</u>, amici! (7 + 1)

3 dominus servo imperavit ut aquam domum <u>ferret</u>. (7 + 1)

139

4 miles tot vulnera acceperat ut mox <u>mortuus sit</u>.   (8 + 1)

5 cives fortiter pugnaverunt ne ab hostibus <u>caperentur</u>.   (7 + 1)

6 nescio cur ille puer hoc <u>fecerit</u>.   (6 + 1)

7 tempestas tam saeva est ut e portu navigare non <u>possimus</u>.   (10 + 1)

8 uxori meae persuadebo ut pecuniam mihi <u>det</u>.   (7 + 1)

9 bene <u>pugnemus</u>, comites!   (3 + 1)

10 magister puerum rogavit quid <u>vellet</u>.   (5 + 1)

Total: 75

Exercise 23.5

1 nuntius, cum haec verba <u>dixisset</u>, discessit.   (6 + 1)

2 ne <u>vincamur</u>!   (2 + 1)

3 puer domum venit ut <u>dormiret</u>.   (5 + 1)

4 magistri discipulis semper imperant ut <u>laborent</u>.   (6 + 1)

5 scio quid <u>facias</u>.   (3 + 1)

6 timebamus ne hostes mox <u>advenirent</u>.   (5 + 1)

7 pueri tam fessi sunt ut <u>dormiant</u>.   (6 + 1)

8 magister, cum sapiens non <u>esset</u>, multa non sciebat.   (8 + 1)

9 laboro ne <u>puniar</u>.   (3 + 1)

10 <u>dormiam</u>!   (1 + 1)

Total: 55

Exercise 23.6

1 nescio cur hoc <u>feceris</u>.   (4 + 1)

2 hic magister tam crudelis est ut discipulos saepe <u>puniat</u>.   (9 + 1)

3 bene <u>pugnemus</u>, milites!   (3 + 1)

4 quis scit quis <u>sit</u>?   (4 + 1)

5 tot hostes erant ut <u>timeremus</u>.   (5 + 1)

6 laboramus ut divites <u>fiamus</u>.   (4 + 1)

7 puella adeo timebat ut <u>fleret</u>.   (5 + 1)

8 pueros hortatus sum ut hoc <u>facerent</u>.   (6 + 1)

9 miles, cum <u>vulneratus esset</u>, non bene pugnabat.   (7 + 1)

10 sciebamus cur <u>currerent</u>.   (3 + 1)

Total: 60

Exercise 23.7

Give the person, number, tense, voice and the 1st person singular of the present indicative active of the following subjunctives:

1 posset.

2 voluisset.

3 inceperit.

4 narraret.

5 sint.

6 loqueretur.

7 eant.

8 deleverit.

9 videres.

10 aedificavissent.

5 marks for each question. Total: 50

Exercise 23.8

Translate the following into English:

1 hic servus a domino cras liberabitur. (6)

2 magistri multa verba saepe dicunt. (5)

3 puella donum amicis ostendit. (4)

4 cur nemo mihi credit? (4)

5 puellam pulchriorem quam illam numquam vidi. (6)

Total: 25

Exercise 24.1

Translate the following passage. Line numbers are given on the left. New words are underlined in the text and their meanings given in the margin.

Penelope and Odysseus are reunited

1 silentium fuit. Penelope corpora procorum,
deinde Ulixem spectavit. ille eam spectabat.
tandem ille 'ego sum Ulixes' inquit, 'rex Ithacae,
coniunx tuus.' Penelope immota manebat.
5 nesciebat utrum hic vir re vera Ulixes esset
necne. eum igitur experiri constituit. 'ancilla,'
clamavit, 'hic vir tam fessus est ut dormire velit.
lectum meum huc adfer!' Ulixes, hoc audito, tam
iratus erat ut clamaverit: 'num lectus meus
10 fractus est, Penelope? ego ipse lectum feci. pars
lecti arbor est. moveri non potest.' Penelope, ut
haec verba audivit, statim scivit hunc virum re
vera Ulixem esse. ad eum cucurrit et amplexa
est. tam laeti erant et Ulixes et Penelope ut flere
15 inceperint. post tot annos una tandem erant.

immotus, -a, -um = motionless

experior, experiri,
expertus, sum (4) = I test
lectus, -i, m. = bed
huc = (to) here
adfero, adferre, attuli,
allatum = I bring (to)
frango, -ere, fregi, fractum
(3) = I break
arbor, arboris, f. = tree
ut + indicative verb = when, as
amplector, amplecti,
amplexus sum (3) = I embrace
una = together

Total: 95

Exercise 24.2

1 From the passage give an example of:

(a) a demonstrative adjective. (1)

(b) a present subjunctive. (1)

2 clamaverit (line 9). In which mood is this verb? Why is this mood used? (2)

3 verba (line 12). In which case is this noun? Why is this case used? (2)

4 inceperint (line 15). Give the tense, mood, voice and 1st person singular of the present indicative active of this verb. (4)

Total: 10

→ Summary of the uses of ut

1 ut + indicative = when, as	servi, **ut** dominum viderunt, fugerunt. **When** they saw the master, the slaves fled. pueri, **ut** scis, numquam laborant. Boys, **as** you know, never work.
2 ut + subjunctive = in order to (purpose clause)	pueri venerunt ut puellas viderent. The boys came **in order to** see the girls.
3 ordering, persuading + ut + subjunctive = to (indirect command)	dux suis imperavit **ut** oppugnarent. The general ordered his men **to** attack.
4 tam, adeo etc + ut+ subjunctive = that, with the result that (consecutive clause)	magister tam ebrius est **ut** ad terram saepe cadat. The teacher is so drunk **that** he often falls to the ground.

Exercise 24.3

Translate the following and explain the use of ut in each sentence:

1 hic miles adeo vulneratus est ut pugnare non posset. (9 + 1)

2 pueri, ut hoc viderunt, riserunt. (5 + 1)

3 mulier filiae imperavit ut curreret. (5 + 1)

4 hic miles tam bene pugnat ut ab hostibus numquam
  vulneretur. (10 + 1)

5 mendicus procos rogabat ut cibum sibi darent. (7 + 1)

6 hi discipuli, ut vides, sapientes non sunt. (7 + 1)

7 puer domum venit ut dormiat. (5 + 1)

8 hic dominus tam dives erat ut multos servos haberet. (9 + 1)

9 milites fortiter pugnaverunt ne ab hostibus vincerentur. (7 + 1)

10 dominus sapiens servo imperavit ne luderet. (6 + 1)

Total: 80

→ Revision

Exercise 24.4

Translate the following into English:

1 dux huic militi imperavit ut bene pugnaret. (7)

2 videre poteram quid ille fecisset. (5)

3 amico meo persuadebo ut librum scribat. (6)

4 amico meo persuasi ut librum scriberet. (6)

5 mulieres timebant ne paucis diebus ab hostibus caperentur. (8)

6 ille senex tam fessus erat ut ambulare non posset. (9)

7 Romani, ut scis, milites optimi erant. (6)

8 miles tot vulnera accepit ut ad terram ceciderit. (8)

9 dux cognoscere volebat ubi copiae hostium essent. (7)

10 puella tam tristis erat ut flere subito inceperit. (8)

Total: 70

Exercise 24.5

Translate the following into English:

1 tantus tumultus in regia erat ut proci passim currerent. (9)

2 omnes scimus Romanos milites optimos esse. (6)

3 proci nesciebant utrum effugere possent necne. (6)

4 Ulixes sciebat lectum suum moveri non posse. (7)

5 cum pauper sim, multum pecuniae non habeo. (7)

6 Ulixes lectum ita aedificaverat ut moveri non posset. (8)

7 spero me illam puellam cras visurum esse. (7)

8 Ulixes nuntiavit se omnes procos occisurum esse. (7)

9 Penelope non credebat hunc virum Ulixem esse. (7)

10 multas puellas in litore iacentes vidi. (6)

Total: 70

Exercise 24.6

Translate the following into English:

1 proci sciebant se effugere non posse. (6)

2 proci sciebant se ab Ulixe interfectum iri. (7)

3 Penelope ancillae imperavit ut lectum moveret. (6)

4 Penelope hoc dixit ut Ulixem experiretur. (6)

5 Graeci multos milites in equo ingenti celaverunt ut urbem
Troiam caperent. (11)

6 Ulixes procos passim currentes spectavit. (5)

7 Troiani tam attoniti erant ut nescirent quid facere deberent. (9)

8 tanta tempestas erat ut naves e portu proficisci non possent. (10)

9 hic magister discipulos semper hortatur ut libros legant. (8)

10 discipuli boni libros legunt ut sapientes fiant. (7)

Total: 75

Exercise 24.7

Translate and name the major construction featured in each of the following sentences:

1 senex nesciebat quis templum aedificavisset. (5 + 1)

2 nescio utrum hunc librum legerim necne. (6 + 1)

3 dux erat tam fortis ut omnes eum laudarent. (8 + 1)

4 uxores viros rogabunt ut sibi dent pecuniam. (7 + 1)

5 dux timebat ne milites capti essent. (6 + 1)

6 pater filium rogavit ut iter secum faceret. (7 + 1)

7 dominus se rogavit quid facere deberet. (6 + 1)

8 te moneo ne hanc aquam bibas. (6 + 1)

9 puer parvus omnes rogavit num parentes vidissent. (7 + 1)

10 dux hostium adeo verebatur ut statim fugerit. (7 + 1)

Total: 75

Exercise 24.8

Translate and name the major construction featured in each of the following sentences:

1 milites rogavit cur tot annos contra Romanos pugnavissent. (8 + 1)

2 Graeci credebant se a Romanis numquam victum iri. (8 + 1)

3 Graeci sciebant se diu pugnare non posse. (7 + 1)

4 Romani progressi sunt ut in hostes ruerent. (7 + 1)

5 mater virum rogavit ne filium malum puniret. (7 + 1)

6 ipse dicit se sapientem esse. (5 + 1)

7 Caesar militibus imperavit ut castra* ponerent. (6 + 1)

8 vos rogo ut hic maneatis. (5 + 1)

9 hic puer tam stultus* est ut nihil sciat. (8 + 1)

10 dic* mihi quis sis! (4 + 1)

*castra, -orum, n. pl. = camp
stultus = stupid
dic = tell!

Total: 75

Exercise 24.9

Double-deckers: translate the following and name the **two** major constructions featured in each sentence:

1 puer patri dixit se timere ne a magistro puniretur.

2 dux dixit se militibus ut oppidum oppugnarent imperaturum esse.

3 dominus villam intravit ut videret utrum servi laborarent necne.

4 omnes discipuli timebant ne magister rogaret cur non laborarent.

5 nuntius celeriter cucurrit ut duci nuntiaret hostes victos esse.

9 + 2 marks for each question. Total: 55

Exercise 24.10

Give the person, number, tense, voice and the 1st person singular of the present indicative active of the following subjunctives:

1 dixerit.

2 poneret.

3 eat.

4 mansissemus.

5 conspicerentur.

6 dederint.

7 pararentur.

8 staret.

9 laudemur.

10 misisses.

5 marks for each question. Total: 50

Exercise 24.11

Translate the following into English:

1 naves e portu prima luce profectae sunt.   (7)

2 viri pauperes multum pecuniae non habent.   (6)

3 multa dona militibus a duce dabantur.   (6)

4 nemo tamen hoc facere poterit.   (5)

5 filia magistri cenam optimam patri parat.   (6)

Total: 30